A History of Highway 60

A History of Highway 60

and the Railroad Towns on the Belen, New Mexico Cutoff

Dixie Boyle

SUNSTONE
PRESS

SANTA FE

Sunstone books may be purchased for educational, business, or sales promotional use.
For information please write: Special Markets Department, Sunstone Press,
P.O. Box 2321, Santa Fe, New Mexico 87504-2321.
Photograph on cover by Marilyn Conway
Book and cover design › Vicki Ahl
Body typeface › Perpetua
Printed on acid-free paper
∞
eBook 978-1-61139-381-1

Library of Congress Cataloging-in-Publication Data

Library of Congress Cataloging-in-Publication Data

Boyle, Dixie, author.
 A history of Highway 60 and the railroad towns on the Belen, New Mexico Cutoff / by
Dixie Boyle.
    pages cm
 Summary: "A History of New Mexico's Highway 60 and the railroad towns on the Belen
Cutoff"--Provided by publisher.
 Includes bibliographical references.
 ISBN 978-1-63293-063-7 (softcover : alk. paper)
 1. New Mexico--History. 2. United States Highway 60--History. 3. Belen (N.M.)--History.
4. Cities and towns--New Mexico--History. I. Title.
 F796.B78 2015
 978.9--dc23
                                    2015017622

WWW.SUNSTONEPRESS.COM
SUNSTONE PRESS / POST OFFICE BOX 2321 / SANTA FE, NM 87504-2321 /USA
(505) 988-4418 / ORDERS ONLY (800) 243-5644 / FAX (505) 988-1025

Dedication

I would like to dedicate this book to the memory of my grandmother Opal Mathews and to my mother Lucille Reynolds. My grandmother rode an emigrant train to New Mexico from Missouri in 1915 and growing up listening to her stories of that time instilled in me a love of history. My mother has always believed in me and supported me in every endeavor I have attempted and I appreciate her support plus her willingness to help conduct interviews and travel Highway 60 with me while researching information for this book.

I would also like to dedicate this book to the memory of Hallie Williams from Negra. I never met Hallie but I have visited her grave, explored the remains of her old house in Negra, walked the same path she did back and forth to the one-room schoolhouse across the road and touched the murals she painted on the walls of Encino's gymnasium. Thank you for inspiring me to tell your story Hallie as well as write the history of Highway 60.

Hallie's murals were destroyed in 2013 when the City of Encino had the old high school and gymnasium torn down due to safety issues. Only a few photographs survive of the beautiful, murals she painted on the walls while teaching math at Encino High School during World War II.

Special thanks to my dear friend Marilyn Conway for taking the cover photograph and others throughout the book.

Thanks to Helen Lavell for sharing her stories and photographs with me, as her stories truly took me back to that wonderful time of train travel when everyone dressed up and ate in elegant dining cars with crystal finger bowls.

Also thanks to Dorothy Cole for sharing her old photographs and stories of Mountainair, New Mexico.

Hallie Williams' Mural. Courtesy: Encino Village Hall. Encino, New Mexico.

Contents

Foreword

Way back in 1980, in a classroom at Hot Springs High School in Truth or Consequences, New Mexico, I had an English teacher who I remember to this day. Her name was Dixie Boyle.

I remember her because she smiled a lot and laughed. I remember her because she cared. I remember her because she was a good teacher, and good teachers are worth remembering.

"Boyle" she told us we could call her that, wanted us all to become writers. So every day in class she'd scribble a thought-provoking question with white chalk on the green chalkboard and give us time to write our answers in our journals while she worked at her desk. One of the questions was, "Why is the Sky Blue?" A tremor of high school angst rippled across the class that day as worry spread that this was actually a science lesson in disguise, until we realized it was just a prompt an invitation to reconsider something we had, to that point, taken for granted. ("The pretty color encourages us to always be looking up," was the gist of my response. I got an A.)

With *A History of Highway 60 and the Railroad Towns on the Belen, New Mexico Cutoff*, Dixie Boyle is at it again, doing what teachers (even former teachers) do best. She's asking questions. She's inviting us to take another look at something so familiar it almost goes unnoticed. It's not the sky this time, but a highway-U.S. 60, running through the meridian of New Mexico, from the Arizona border through Magdalena and Socorro and Mountainair and Clovis to the Texas border. In each chapter, Dixie explores the history of a community along the way and the lives of the rugged individuals who settled these places. Here are stories of Charles Lindbergh's emergency landing outside Vaughn, the delicious pies of Pie Town, the ghost towns of Negra and Pedernal, and the heyday of pinto bean farming in the Estancia Valley. Great stories, so often untold!

But underneath all this, Dixie is asking us questions, questions about our past and our obligation to it, questions about our connections to the places we live and to one another, questions about how a stretch of unmoving, unchanging blacktop can, to paraphrase a familiar philosophy, never be the same road twice.

I can almost see her back in that classroom writing today's journal question on the green chalkboard: "Can a highway have a soul?"

Motivated by the changes she saw in this part of New Mexico, and mourning the stories that were being lost with the passing of each generation, Dixie fought back, with words, with awareness. She became a highway historian—a Road Scholar—talking to people, researching, documenting. This is, after all, her country. Dixie grew up in Mountainair and later taught school there. She went to a homecoming dance in Encino. She listened to her father's stories about this part of the state as they drove along U.S. 60 over the endless plains of the Llano Estacado.

Focusing on a highway that, in her words, "most people only travel to get somewhere else," Dixie wrote a book that encourages us to drop the "else." It is as much a travel guide as it is a history textbook as it is a defense against the march of time. It succeeds on all three levels.

I met up with Dixie Boyle again in the summer of 2014 in a firetower high atop the Manzano Mountains, where she works summers as a fire lookout. The tower is the highest point for hundreds of miles and offers a view that is half earth and half sky. It's an appropriate workplace for someone so adept at seeing the big picture. She's probably up there right now as you're reading this, following the line of Highway 60 with her eye as it winds away toward the horizon in both directions. The highway and the people who live along it, have no greater advocate than "Boyle."

So, the question remains. Can a highway have a soul?

I think Dixie's book provides a convincing answer.

—David Pike, author of *Roadside New Mexico*
February 2015

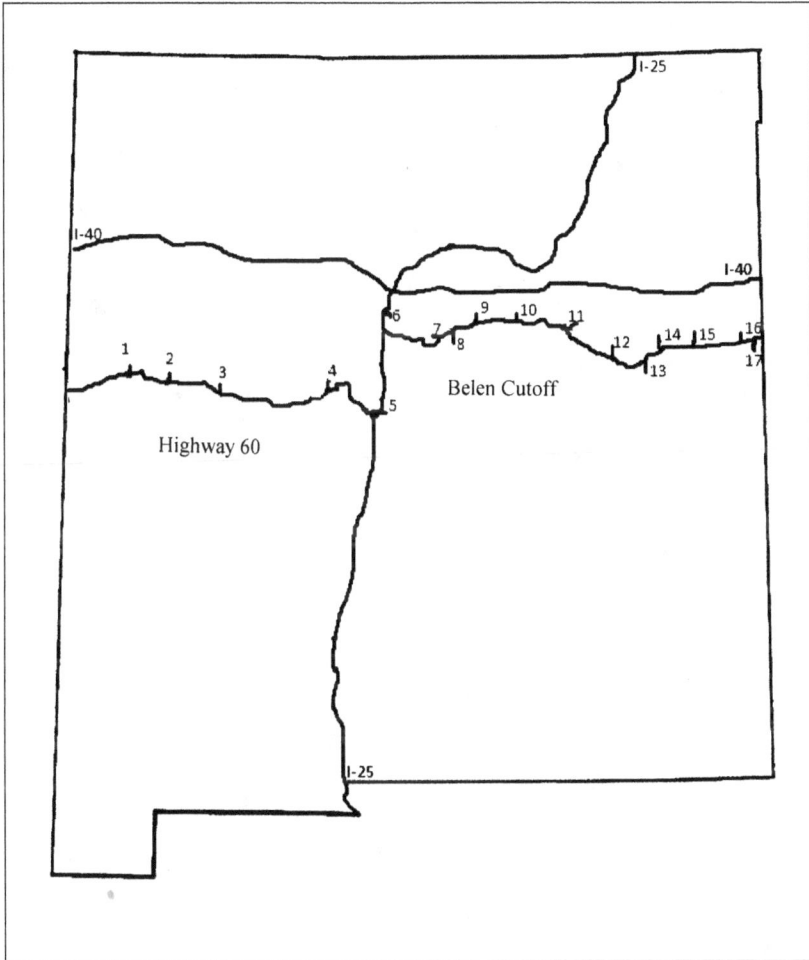

Map of New Mexico

Towns along Highway 60 and the Belen Cutoff: 1. Quemado, 2. Pie Town, 3. Datil, 4. Magdalena, 5. Socorro, 6. Belen , 7. Scholle and Abo, 8. Mountainair, 9. Willard, 10. Lucy, 11. Pedernal, 12. Negra and Encino, 13. Vaughn, 14. Yeso and Fort Sumner, 15. Tolar, Taiban and Melrose, 16. Clovis, 17. Texico.

Preface

The American frontier was populated by ambitious dreamers who possessed the drive, determination and foresight to see their dreams become a reality. Cyrus Holliday had such a dream about a transcontinental railroad. In January of 1859 he wrote a charter for the Atchison, Topeka & Santa Fe (AT&SF) Railroad.

The charter provided for a railroad from Atchison, Kansas on the Missouri River to either the southern or eastern boundary of the territory of Santa Fe and a branch line to the Gulf of Mexico. The Civil War and extreme drought delayed construction, but Holliday never stopped working to ensure the development of the railroad. Ten years later in 1869 the line had only been extended seven miles but Holliday supplied crackers and a keg of beer for those riding the train to the end of the track in celebration of its construction.

Soon the AT&SF began building track westward. As the railroad crossed the country, the depot and stockyards soon became the center of town. Saloons and brothels sprang up and many of these early railroad towns were violent with numerous gunfights and brawls. The railroad was more interested in making money during the early years and spent time working on their stockyards for the massive herds of cattle that would soon be arriving at the railheads for shipment to Chicago and the East coast.

Holliday and his crew supervisors had problems with the crews laying track in these cattle towns and rushed through as quickly as possible to a site a few miles from the town. There were times when they lost most of their crew in the saloons and bordellos and had to search for others to work in their place.

The end of the track arrived in Dodge City, Kansas in 1872 and the crews continued toward the Colorado border with amazing endurance. After crossing Colorado they narrowly won the right-of-way through Raton Pass in 1878 and continued to the southwest reaching Las Vegas, NM in 1879. By 1880 the tracks passed through Albuquerque and arrived in San Marcial south of Socorro in September extending the track two hundred and thirty five miles from Las Vegas. The AT&SF made it to the West coast in October of 1882 twenty-three years after the organization of the railroad company.

During his day, the Fred Harvey name represented the finest in railroad dining with efficient waitresses and appealing hotel accommodations. Prior to this time, railroad lunch counters possessed inedible food and passengers often did not have time to eat the meal once they were purchased. Most cooks had worked in logging and mining camps and on cattle drives and did not care about the elegance of their setting or the appearance of their food.

Most menus during this era in lunch counter dining consisted of rancid bacon, canned beans and eggs. Sinkers were a common name for soda biscuits and the menu topped off with either cold tea or bitter black coffee.

There were no napkins on the table and the table cloths were often dirty with broken and chipped china. The waiters during this era were called hash slingers. Lunch stops were generally only twenty minutes. Often restaurant and train crews would signal lunch time was over before the passenger had a chance to eat and then divided the profits of the uneaten and untouched meal. Then the process started over again when the next train arrived. Most of the passengers brought their own lunches or purchased sandwiches on the train from attendants called "butcher boys."

Before Fred Harvey's time there were not many dining cars in the East and none in the West. There were few eating establishments near the tracks and it was common for the engineer and train crews to cook their own meals at the roundhouse or boiler room at the end of their shift.

The Santa Fe Railroad tried a lunch counter at the Topeka Depot in 1874 but it was not successful because railroad employees found the food distasteful. But, when Fred Harvey leased the Topeka Lunch Counter two years later, their attitudes changed and the railroad company decided lunch counters might be a good idea.

Harvey was born in England in 1835 and migrated to the United States when he was fifteen years old. When he arrived in New York City he found a job as a busboy at a café for two dollars a week. The work did not hold his attention and he moved on to New Orleans and then St. Louis, Missouri where he took a position with the Chicago, Burlington & Quincy Railroad as the western freight agent for the railroad company.

Afterwards, Fred Harvey and the AT&SF formed an agreement to provide restaurants and accommodations at specific sites on the line. Harvey had to be creative at times but believed railroad passengers and workers deserved better food than they were receiving along the route. At his first lunch counters he ordered pies to be cut into four pieces instead of the traditional six and used cloth napkins and better silverware. Most businesses of the era did not have the standards possessed by Fred Harvey.

Harvey had most of his problems with unruly customers on New Mexico's portion of the route. Cowboys had a practice of shooting and hurrahing the town, meaning they shot out windows of the local businesses and shot their guns in the air while riding at a fast speed. They yelled and screamed announcing their presence in town.

While working at the Montezuma Harvey House in Las Vegas a group of drunken cowboys came into Harvey's establishment and immediately started to shoot up the billiard room. Harvey followed the group into the bar where they shot at a collection of Native American artifacts and bottles of expensive alcohol behind the bar.

Harvey shouted at them to stop what they were doing and to act like gentlemen and they could only stay if they paid for their drinks. He asked them to put away their guns and have a drink with him, but one of the cowboys started cussing so the story goes and Harvey jerked him by the collar over the bar and held him down on the floor. The cowboy finally agreed to not use profane language in Harvey's establishment.

In Lamy gamblers and outlaws took over the town, refused to pay for their food and stole the money intended for the payroll for the Harvey House employees. They planned on hanging the manager of the Harvey House but Harvey was able to talk them out of it.

Harvey's waitresses were known as Harvey Girls. Harvey and his dining establishments are credited with civilizing the West and serving food in a graceful manner. Harvey felt it was important to have the food waiting for the passengers when they entered the depot. Each Harvey House received between four to five trains each day.

The managers of Harvey Houses along the route advertised for young women between the ages of 18 and 30 years old and sought those who were attractive and intelligent. They had to agree not to marry for one year. Starting wage for a Harvey Girl was $17.50 a week plus tips room and board. They wore black shoes and stockings, plain black dresses and heavily starched white aprons and their hair was adorned with a white ribbon. Most of the Harvey Girls remained in one location throughout their careers but others enjoyed moving from one location to another along the railroad route.

Fred Harvey and his staff constantly reviewed their menus and changed them when needed. He also sold Native American arts and crafts, rugs, jewelry, blankets, turquoise beads and silver work and was one of the first to do so. He was truly ahead of his time and made railroad dining a luxury.

Raton Pass with a three percent grade caused trains to run double-headed, meaning there was an engine on the front and another at the rear of the train providing enough power to ascend the pass. By 1900, traffic over Raton Pass caused a serious bottleneck and slowed operations throughout the state. The AT&SF began looking for a more direct route to the Pacific. When the railroad company acquired the Pecos Railroad line and its extension to Amarillo, Texas, there only remained a gap from the Texas border to Belen in central New Mexico. Upon completion of the line to fill this gap all the AT&SF tracks would be connected.

In 1903 a construction contract was awarded to Lantry & Sons a firm from Kansas. A large work force was hired to lay track to Abo Pass. Almost instantly Belen began to boom as the railroad employed seventy-five freight teams to supply five railroad camps east of town.

Due to financial instability in the stock market the construction of the railroad was halted in July of 1903. Twenty miles of rail had been laid east of Belen and much of the grading to the summit of Abo Pass completed. Work would not resume until August of 1905 and by January of the following year there were three hundred men working on the railway line. Crews laid two hundred and forty nine miles of track between Texico and Belen and this line became known as the Belen Cutoff and is still one of the more lucrative freight lines the railroad has.

Towns quickly came to life beside the tracks. One town named Sunnyside later known as Fort Sumner was created when the Eastern Railway was completed in March of 1906. Sunnyside boasted seven saloons, three restaurants and hundreds of tent homes. In the town's early history there were more saloons and bordellos than other businesses.

At the turn of the twentieth century, the AT&SF and other railroad companies laid out towns, depots and division sites along the proposed Belen Cutoff. This became one of the largest land grabs in the history of New Mexico.

The AT&SF organized a campaign in 1908 to settle New Mexico's eastern plains. Posters left along the line described town sites and homesteading opportunities on the Belen Cutoff. The homesteaders came by the train loads in 1908 with two or three families aboard. Most homesteaders came from Kansas, Missouri, Oklahoma and Texas.

Unknown couple riding train on the Belen Cutoff. Courtesy: Dorothy Cole Collection.

Many of the smaller towns along the cutoff slowly died after the passenger service ended. Prior to this the railroad provided transportation for people living in the isolated communities and the depots were lively spots where the mail and packages were delivered and people met to visit and catch up on the news of their neighbors. In most cases even the depots were moved when the passenger service ended.

All the railroad depots along the Belen Cutoff were built in 1908, reflecting the power of the railroad to bring life to what was once nothing but vacant land. They were built of adobe brick with arched breezeways for cooling during New Mexico's hot summers. There were few places to live on the frontier when the railroad first came through, so the railroad solved their housing problems by providing living quarters on the second floor of the depot. The upstairs housed traveling railroad workers as well as those stationed in the area.

Centralized traffic control was installed in the 1940s and in 1944 the roundhouse at Clovis and Belen were extended to accommodate larger loco-motives. Early passenger trains on the route were the Scout and Missionary models. The route continues as a freight line with trains passing through every ten to fifteen minutes.

Highway 60 follows the route of the Belen Cutoff through eastern and central New Mexico before crossing the Rio Grande River and Continental Divide on its way to Arizona. The highway is nicknamed the coast-to-coast or ocean-to-ocean highway. The route originally began in Virginia Beach on the Atlantic Coast and ended at the Pacific Ocean in Los Angeles. The highway crosses the Appalachian and Ozark Mountains, the Great Plains and American Southwest on its way to the West coast.

At the turn of the twentieth century Henry Ford's invention of the first automobile triggered a desire for transcontinental travel among Amer-icans. Those states west of the Mississippi River were not ready or equipped for this type travel, as only freight and wagon roads crisscrossed much of what was left of the American frontier. The first automobile travelers had more adventures crossing the roads than traveling through the towns. Most pioneer auto travelers transported food, water and items for camping.

In 1910 the National Highway Association laid out an auto route across the nation from coast to coast. A.L. Westgard was hired to make a trip in search of the best route. He followed various routes west from Washington, D.C. to Kansas City and along the route of the Santa Fe Trail. He searched for the best river crossings and topography suiting a transcontinental highway.

In 1911 Westgard made a second trip, and this time followed the Rio Grande River to Socorro then to the West through Magdalena, Datil, Pie Town, Quemado and Springerville, Arizona. He back-tracked to Los Lunas but found the only roads westward from there were freight and wagon roads and not fit for automobile traffic. The route through Magdalena to the Arizona border was the most direct route across the state. By 1918 Highway 60 emerged from a wagon road to a primitive truck route.

Present-day Highway 60 has been rerouted since the original highway was laid out. In the beginning, it was a dirt road with few conveniences along the route. Often times horses, wagons and early vehicles were all lined up on early streets as shown in this 1916 photograph of Mountainair's Main Street.

Mountainair in 1916. Courtesy: Dorothy Cole Collection.

The romance years of traveling by train have passed. All the Harvey Houses along the route have been converted into museums or restaurants, destroyed by fire or abandoned. Most Americans have forgotten the Harvey Girls and the American public has left trains behind for the convenience of flying. Few people living today remember the Harvey House Restaurants or the luxurious, dining cars that came after.

Ninety-four year old Helen Lavell remembers riding the AT&SF trains from Topeka, Kansas to Los Angeles, California in the 1920s. Her family often traveled to California on vacation and she has fond memories of her train riding days.

Helen's father John Meyer was an instructor at the Topeka Apprentice School sponsored by the AT&SF Railroad. In the railroad's infancy, it was often found there were few skilled laborers and in an attempt to fill that gap, the Santa Fe sponsored apprentice schools in most of the larger towns along the route.

588 - Santa Fe Depot, Topeka, Kan.

Santa Fe Depot in Topeka, Kansas. Author's collection.

In an article by F. W. Thomas titled *Educating Apprentice on the Santa Fe*, "The present apprentice system had its birth when the road was in crying need of skilled mechanics. Work was in abundance but the laborers were few."

At first the Santa Fe set aside a building or room where railroad workers met and learned the mechanics of running a railroad. Thomas wrote, "The apprentice was required to spend two hours a day two days a week where he is taught free-hand and mechanical drawing, practical shop arithmetic, the simpler element of mechanics and certain geography and history relating to the road."

Harvey Houses were in full service along the track during these years and Lavell relates a story about stopping for lunch on the route, "Everyone ate at the Harvey Houses in those days, as it was the best food to be found. We were rushed through and our meals were still hot and ready when we arrived," she stated in a telephone interview.

Fred Harvey was the first to have Native American jewelry and silver work for sale near the tracks outside the Harvey Houses. Lavell describes buying jewelry for the first time, "When we got off the train there was turquoise, silver and beaded jewelry on display by different Native American tribes and most of us could not resist purchasing a piece or two," replied Lavell. "It was so different from anything we had seen before."

Lavell enjoyed riding in the Pullman cars, where there were bunks stacked on top of one another for sleeping with a large bathroom and nice sinks and compartments. "Sometimes my dad would allow us to ride on the open back end of the train and enjoy the view, and there was also an official open air car we frequented when needing air or wanting to watch the scenery," she explained.

Most Harvey Houses throughout the country were out of business by 1939. A major contributing factor to their demise was the introduction of the Super Chief in 1937, a streamlined first class passenger train operated by a diesel locomotive. The AT&SF painted the front of the train in its famous "Warbonnet" colors and it was soon recognized throughout the world.

The new Super Chief operated between Los Angeles and Chicago and was nicknamed the "Train of the Stars" because of the many Hollywood personalities riding the train. It took a little under forty hours to travel between Chicago and Los Angeles in the 1930s which was the fastest way to cross the country. The movie stars frequenting the train also added to its popularity. In the 1940s Lionel toys created toy trains in the "Warbonnet" colors, and they too soon became popular throughout the United States causing more travelers to use the train.

According to an article in *On Track* published by the California State Railroad Museum Foundation, "The Super Chief's marketing slogan Extra Fine-Extra Fast-Extra Fare was taken very seriously by the railroad. Yes, the trip cost passengers a pretty penny, but in this pre-jet airplane era, it got them to their destination quickly and in style."

The Super Chief also introduced elegant, dining cars where passengers could eat and sleep on the train as they traveled across the country. Although, the move was good for the railroad company it would not be so for the remaining Harvey Houses.

Santa Fe Super Chief in Albuquerque. Author's collection.

"I loved dining on the cars as they were so elegant with linen table cloths, china finger bowls and served by waiters wearing white jackets," related Lavell. "The dining rooms were very comfortable and you could watch the landscape as you were eating."

Lavell and her family usually traveled first class, but for those who could not afford a first class ticket, travelers could purchase what was known as a chair car ticket. "Most of those riding in the chair cars brought their own food or purchased sandwiches from waiters on the train," she pointed out. "If we were traveling a short distance we traveled on the chair car."

For those who could afford train travel, it was the quickest and most comfortable method of transportation. "Everyone traveled by train in those days, as it was the only way to go. There were few airports or planes during these years and most railroad depots were busy and interesting places," Lavell replied. "Even the local baseball teams rode the train in what we referred to as baseball cars. They were always a happy and noisy group."

During this era in railroad history train depots and terminals were built in the Victorian style with cupolas, dormers and long platforms. Some of the counters were constructed of marble. "It was fun arriving at the grand depots of the 1920s. Everyone dressed up to ride the train," stated Lavell. "The women were adorned in their best dresses and hats and my father wore a suit when we traveled on the train. There was always a festive feeling at the train depot. There were gift shops, shoe-shine stands and people visiting and moving throughout the depot with trains arriving and departing."

Romero family dressed up to ride the train in Mountainair.
Courtesy: Dorothy Cole Collection.

Train travel began to decline during World War II as most Americans possessed automobiles and planes were available for cross country travel. Rail travel peaked in the 1920s and then went downhill after that. When President Eisenhower signed the Interstate Highway System act into effect in 1956 this sealed the fate of train travel. Amtrack would become the more popular mode of train travel starting in 1971.

The AT&SF or Santa Fe as it was more affectionately called was merged with the Burling Northern Railroad in 1996 and the railroad line is now known as the Burling Northern & Santa Fe Railroad (BNSF).

"The railroad era has passed and now Americans can make it across the United States in a few hours instead of days," Lavell commented. "But, the elegance of early train travel will never return and I still miss it at times."

Helen Lavell riding the train with her parents in 1925. Courtesy: Helen Lavell.

1

Belen, Felipe Chavez and John Becker

The community of Belen meaning Bethlehem in Spanish was mentioned in historical records after the Pueblo Revolt of 1680 when the settlement was destroyed. Formal settlement of the town began in 1740 when Diego de Torrez and Antonio de Salazar petitioned for the land grant known as Nuestra de Senor de Belen. Settlement persisted for hundreds of years before the Apache and other tribes were subdued and Europeans began settling along the Rio Grande River.

The original land grant was two hundred thousand acres and extended from the Rio Grande River to the Manzano Mountains. Los Chavez was the boundary to the north and Bernardo to the south. In 1750 a military garrison was established for the protection of the haciendas and missions along the river.

Even during the Spanish colonization period, Belen was known as the Hub as it was surrounded by early Spanish villages along the river. Some of these early villages were: La Joya, Bosque, Pueblitos, Los Trujillo and Jarales. Each of these communities had their own plazas and made their living by trading on the Camino Real or Royal Road from Mexico City to Santa Fe.

Tome and Los Lunas to the north of Belen were early settlements in the area too. Many residents from Tome spread to Socorro and across the Manzano Mountains to the east. Don Domingo was one of the first of the Luna family to settle in what would become New Mexico. In 1692, Don Domingo was awarded a land grant surrounding present-day Los Lunas and beyond. Over a hundred years later, the AT&SF Railroad proposed building line through the Luna's hacienda. The family agreed, if the railroad would replace the hacienda. Today, their home is known as the Luna Mansion and is a popular historic restaurant in Los Lunas.

For thirty years the residents of Valencia County had a hard time deciding where they wanted their county seat. The seat of county government was in Valencia in 1846 but moved to Peralta in 1847. Next the residents voted to return the county seat to Valencia in 1849 and then to Tome in 1850. Twenty years later Belen was awarded the county seat status for a short time but lost to Tome in 1874. In 1875 the citizens finally made up their minds and awarded the county seat to Los Lunas where it has remained.

Felipe Chavez was the richest merchant in Belen in the 1840s. Chavez nicknamed El Millionario was a politician, rancher and philanthropist. Legends tell of him drying his gold and silver in the Chavez plaza. Chavez launched his first business venture on North Main Street where the Walgreen's Drugstore is currently located and his store soon became known for its wide variety of merchandise. The store also had an extra, long bar with Mexican silver coins embedded in it.

Felipe Chavez married his first cousin Josefa Chavez, a common practice among the old Spanish families in order to keep the wealth in the family. Felipe Chavez was born in 1835 at Los Padillas to one of the oldest and most powerful families in the state.

Chavez was a judge in Belen for a number of years and built a small jail in the courtyard behind his house. He would sentence criminals and those rustling cattle to death and then walk them a few feet to a cottonwood tree where they were hanged for their crimes. He dispensed frontier justice as soon as possible.

Chavez lent John Becker money when he first arrived in town and they soon formed a friendship and worked together for the good of the town. The two men are responsible for the AT&SF Railroad launching the Belen Cutoff from their community. Chavez was a major stockholder in the railroad company and Becker donated land for the depot and Harvey House.

In the 1880s the Rio Grande Valley was nicknamed "The Land of Opportunity" from as far away as Germany. Many Europeans settled in the area and their names remain: Sachs, Goebels, Scholles, Hunings, John Becker and Felipe Chavez. They all started mercantile stores and brought stability and commerce to the towns along the Rio Grande River.

John Becker emigrated from the Province of Hanover in Germany arriving in New York City in 1869 where he made arrangements to travel to New Mexico Territory. His uncle Louis Huning was holding a job in his mercantile store in Los Lunas for him and encouraged Becker to travel to the United States. After a few months Huning turned over the Belen store to Becker. He was later able to establish his own store in Belen in 1879. It quickly developed into one of the most popular department stores of its day where dry good and grocery items could be purchased.

In November of 1877 John Becker was united in marriage to Ann Vielstitch, who was also a native of Germany. They had six children who would become involved in the mercantile business. His children's names were: Hans, Louie, Anna, Gustav, Lucie and Bernhart. The family attended the Lutheran Church and was a good influence in the growing community.

Most of the Becker children went into the family business their father had started. Becker built his daughter Lucie a two-story house west of his store and next to the Becker house. It seems, not only would the family dine with Lucie during lunch time most days but the store's extensive staff was also invited.

Anna Becker spent long hours working in her husband's store as did most members of the large family. She learned to speak the Spanish language as soon as possible after her arrival in New Mexico Territory, as John Becker insisted that all of his employees learn to speak the local language. Anna Becker passed away ten years before her husband.

As early as 1904 Becker had plotted land for a city park in Belen, and his only request concerning the park was that it be named after his wife Anna Becker. Previous to the construction of the park, Becker had used the area as a pond to drain off excess water from his irrigated fields. During these years, it was referred to as the Belen Pond and used by the community as an ice skating ring during the winter months.

In 1934 the community decided to use the area for a town park and back filled the pond before starting construction. The park has been a favorite location for Belen residents for over eighty years. After its initial construction it was used for baseball games, family activities and in the early years there were band concerts in the park on most Saturday evenings.

All of Anna's sisters also moved to Belen and married men who worked for John Becker. Johanna married John's brother, Frederick, Meta married Carl Dailes and Katherine married Bernhard Reinken.

Becker's store was similar to Chavez' early mercantile store and carried a little of everything. The store carried firewood, groceries, hardware, furniture, clothing, shoes, boots, gas, oil, grease, alcohol, hay, lumber, livestock feed and in later years tractors, automobiles and caskets.

Not only was Becker instrumental in attracting the railroad to Belen, but shortly after his arrival he decided to update the flour mill as it was run down and not operating at a optimum level. He eventually constructed a full roller process flour mill that was operated by steam power. Soon farmers were taking most of their wheat to Becker and he was turning out one hundred barrels of flour each day.

The AT&SF Railroad considered a route through Tijeras Canyon east of Albuquerque, but Chavez and Becker had pull and convinced the railroad to construct the line through Belen instead. A Harvey House was built near the tracks in 1910.

The Belen Harvey House is one of the few original Harvey Houses remaining in New Mexico. Luckily, the majestic, old building was converted into a museum in 1985 and much of its history has been preserved.

Belen Harvey House. Author's collection.

The Belen Harvey House was built at a cost of twenty five thousand dollars. The lunch room had a marble, lunch counter, fine linen, crystal and silver. According to the Belen Harvey House brochure, "Swinging double-leaf wood doors connected the lunchroom to the kitchen. Oak wainscoting decorated the lunchroom and the dining room walls, and stained-glass panels graced the window transoms. The dining room floor was oak; the lunchroom floor was octagonal tile."

Harvey Houses closed along the Belen Cutoff in 1939 including the Belen Harvey House and Las Chavez in Vaughn. The passengers were not eating in the Harvey Houses as they had in the past due to the railroad's experiment with dining cars. The economical upheaval throughout the United States during the depression and war years did not help the Harvey Houses to remain in business. The Belen Harvey House did open again for a short time in 1943 to serve troops riding the trains during World War II. Between the years of 1954 and 1978 the building was used as a reading room and rooming house for railroad workers.

The Belen Harvey House might have been demolished like the other houses in the state if the people of Belen had not made an effort to save their Harvey House. According to the Belen Harvey House brochure, "After being boarded up and readied for demolition, a campaign by local citizens and the city saved the building from being torn down. The AT&SF donated the property to the City of Belen in 1982. With the help of the Valencia County Historical Society and hundreds of volunteers, restoration on the building and grounds began."

The Harvey House reopened in 1985 as a civic center. Office space was available for non-profit groups and government offices. Activities provided by the civic center took a toll on the old building and those in charge decided to have the space completely converted into a Harvey House Museum.

In 2013 the Valencia County Historical Society decided to turn over management of the museum and its collection to the City of Belen and the Belen Public Library. A new branch library according to the museum brochure now specializes in Harvey House, railroad and Southwest history.

The museum has also extended its hours. The Harvey House is open on Tuesday between 9:00 a.m. and 4:00 p.m. Wednesday through Saturday the museum is open between the hours of 12:30 p.m. and 4:00 p.m. and is closed Sunday and Monday.

Belen was incorporated in 1918 and became a town in 1940 and a city in 1966. The railroad remains a major employer. One hundred and ten trains travel through Belen in a twenty-four hour period. The railroad depot and Harvey House are in the center of town as a reminder of the AT&SF Railroad's significance and contributions to the growth of the area. The population of Belen in the 2013 census was seven thousand two hundred and thirty nine residents.

2

Scholle and Abo

Abo Ruins. Courtesy: Marilyn Conway Photography.

Located thirteen miles west of Mountainair, Scholle was named after a pioneer mercantile owner from Belen who used the area to herd his vast flocks of sheep. When the railroad established a watering station at the site, Fred Scholle sold the land and left his name for the railroad town that followed. The community had become a boom town by 1916.

Scholle would boom for forty years until the railroad downsized and closed the depot and railroad yard. When trucks became the standard vehicle used for shipping, the railroad yard was used for holding the cattle before loading them on the trucks. In later years, cattle buyers made even the railroad yard obsolete.

Dances were held twice a week and lasted all night. Cake and coffee were served at a midnight intermission where women's reputations were judged by their cakes, even though they might have ridden horseback or in a wagon all afternoon in order to make it to the dance at sundown. Scholle was famous for its square dances. Many dances were held at the schoolhouse and others at a dancehall built by Canuto Sisneros. The town survived into the 1950s although the school closed in 1946 and the remaining students bussed into Mountainair.

The community's most well-known resident was Joe J. Brazil. Born and raised in Scholle in 1924, he spent the majority of his life there raising cattle. Referred to as a poet and philosopher, he was also an accomplished artist. While serving in the South Pacific during World War II, he made enough money drawing portraits of his fellow soldiers and painting on B-24 bomber planes to start his first cattle herd when he returned home. He continued drawing in his spare time, and became an accomplished artist of ranch scenes and Western life. He died in his home outside Scholle in 2006.

The Brazil brothers arrived in the United States from the Azore Mountains in Portugal and homesteaded land near Scholle. The parents of Joe J. were Jose Joaquin and Marie Espinosa. They were married in 1917 and soon began adding land to their ranch in Scholle and becoming prominent ranchers in the area.

Clarence Pohl moved to Scholle shortly after 1900 and established the first store in 1917. The store would later serve as the post office until the demise of the town forty years later. The first settlers were the Garcias, Marshalls, Contreras, Kaysers, Brazils, Pohls and the Sisneros families.

The first school used in the small community was a railroad boxcar, but the town eventually built a school building on the north side of Highway 60. The school, Clarence Pohl's post office and the ruins of Joe J. Brazil's home and artist studio are all that remain of Scholle. The central part of the community consisted of Pohl's store, a dance hall, freight depot station and during the booming years loading pens for livestock.

Early settlers along Forest Road 422 west of Scholle often traveled between the Manzano Mountains and the railroad settlements to buy supplies and seek entertainment. Forest Road 422 travels through Priest Canyon. The canyon has also gone by the name of La Saladas and the Padilla Ranch in its earlier history. The southern end of the Manzano Mountains was also used for sheep grazing in its early years and as was the Los Pinos Range to the south.

The Padilla family was another of the early Spanish settlers to establish a home near what would become Highway 60. They came from La Joya along the Rio Grande River and at first settled at La Cienega, west of Punta de Agua. Later Gabino Padilla and his three sons homesteaded land at the head of Priest Canyon. A small community formed and during this era was referred to as the Padilla Ranch.

The community had its own school known as the Valencia County School but it closed in 1947. The Padilla family had to move in order to find work after the U.S. Forest Service made it part of the Manzano National Forest Reserve in 1905. On early U.S. Forest Service maps the area is called Priest Canyon, supposedly after a crumbling adobe structure near the boundary where a priest once lived.

---- -

The location of Abo has become a ghost town more than once during its one thousand year history. For centuries after the Tompiro Indians abandoned the site in the 1670s due to drought and Apache raids, no one settled at Abo Pass.

Mogollon pithouses dotted the landscape at Abo Pass as early as 950 and the site of Abo was first occupied in 1150. By 1400 the Tompiro had made the site a pottery trade center, and a Spanish census lists fifteen hundred people living at Abo in 1640. But, by the 1670s Navajo and Apache raids plus continuous drought and disease had made life at the pueblo impossible and Abo was abandoned.

The Tompiros often traveled to the Rio Grande River to trade with those following the Camino Real between Mexico City and Santa Fe. Accomplished farmers, the Tompiro tended orchards of peaches, apples, and apricots, as well as fields of corn and squash.

The land between the Rio Grande River and Llano Estacado on New Mexico's east side was inhabited by Comanche, Apache and Navajo Indians when the first settlers arrived on the eastern slopes of the Manzano Mountains. For centuries before that the Tompiro constructed pueblos in the vicinity and endured the Spanish invasion of the 1600s.

Belen, Bernalillo, Sabinal, Tome and Valencia were among the earliest settlements on the west side of the Manzano Range. Sheepherders used the area for grazing as early as 1703, but formal settlement of Manzano was not established until one hundred and sixty people from Tome moved to the site in 1824.

The first Spanish colonists to build permanent settlements near Abo and on the west side of the Manzano Mountains, built their settlements in the style of a plazuela or fortified town with walls surrounding the community and a torreon for protection. A torreon was normally a round structure with portholes for shooting where the settlers could lock themselves inside and wait out an Apache attack. During these years, this type of structure was common as it was a way the Spanish settlers found they could survive Apache and Navajo raids.

Water, supplies and ammunition were stored inside the torreon and during an Apache raid the women and children remained inside while the men fought off the Apache outside. Someone was always on guard watching for an attack while the others worked in their fields. Those first Spanish settlers were a tough and determined group.

Between the years of 1815 and 1830, the Sisneros, Pino, Lucero, Baca and Sanchez families were the first to attempt settling the land near Abo Pass and the ancient Tompiro site. They brought their families and sheep. After fifteen years of Apache and Comanche raids, they decided to move closer to

Manzano, where there was more protection. But they could not forget about their former home, and returned thirty six years later. Their descendants continue to live in the area.

At a different location a few miles southeast of the Tompiro ruins on the south side of Highway 60 are the remains of the railroad town of Abo. A four-room schoolhouse, in session between 1913 and 1960, is testament to its once thriving status, although the town started to decline when the railroad retired its depot in 1940. During its heyday the community also supported two saloons, a post office, and a Catholic Church, still occasionally in use for funerals and weddings.

An interesting pioneer from Abo was Maude Medders who moved to the area in 1917 as the new bride of Will Medders. They raised a family of seven children, grew pinto beans and ranched for the remainder of their lives together. She broke horses and lived a peaceful life giving no hint of the terror and heartbreak she had experienced when she was a young bride on the Mexican frontier.

In 1916 Ed and Maude Wright were ranching near Pearson, Mexico two hundred miles from the United States border when raiders under the command of Pancho Villa took them captive. Ed and a friend named Ed Hayden had gone to Pearson for supplies and Maud was fixing dinner when she heard horses. Before she could reach the door Villa's soldiers kicked it in and entered the house. They demanded food and took what food supplies the Wrights had left.

Ed and Hayden returned shortly after the raiders arrived. They were surrounded, their wagon load of supplies confiscated along with the livestock. They were forced at gunpoint to mount their horses and accompany the raiders. Their two-year old son was left behind with a Mexican family employed by the Wrights.

At a junction near the ranch, Ed and Hayden were taken behind a bluff and killed. Maude heard shots and knew they were dead when the soldiers returned with only the horses. She tried to escape, but Villa threatened to kill her if she tried again. She remained his prisoner for nine days as there were few opportunities to escape and she knew Villa would kill her if she tried again.

When Villa invaded the United States during the Columbus Raid, Maude was left with the soldiers guarding the horses. After Villa's army was defeated he returned and told Maude to pick up a stick, tie a light cloth on it and wave while riding into Columbus. She was taken into custody by U.S. soldiers at Columbus and turned over to Colonel Slocum where she was interrogated about spying for Pancho Villa. She was eventually cleared and allowed to pick up her infant son in El Paso before moving to Safford, Arizona and reuniting with her parents.

At eighty-one years old she rode a mule to the top of the Manzano Mountains proving she could still outride even her grandchildren. She quietly lived the remainder of her life as the binding force behind her family as did pioneer ranch women throughout New Mexico.

Abo with its colorful mesas and history has attracted retirees, artists and ranchers over the past few decades. Many of the larger ranches south of Abo have remained in the same families for a hundred years after the Homestead Act encouraged settlement of the area. Salinas Pueblo Missions National Monument is now in charge of the ancient pueblo at Abo a popular destination for historians, travelers and those seeking a quiet place to eat their lunch under the cottonwood trees.

3

Mountainair, the Pinto Bean Capital of the World

Pinto beans and homesteaders put Mountainair on the map by 1918 as the Pinto Bean Capital of the World. Starting in 1911 with the first bean shipment and continuing through the 1940s, bean elevators in Mountainair processed more pinto beans than any other in Torrance County or elsewhere in the world. The wet climate and virgin fields provided more pinto beans than the farmers could process before the drought years hit.

Mountainair Trading Company. Courtesy: Dorothy Cole Collection.

The Mountainair Trading Company established in 1917 soon had the biggest store and bean elevator in town. The Trinidad Bean & Elevator Company from Colorado built elevators in Colorado and New Mexico and had their largest elevator in Mountainair. The Trinidad Company opened in 1918 and closed in 1945. The bean elevators and trucks bringing pinto beans to be processed caused a bustling farming atmosphere in the community when farmers came into town from all parts of the county on Saturday mornings.

Pictures surviving from that era show women in fashionable hats and dresses walking the streets with their family and friends.

Shirley Willis gives an account in the *Torrance County History* book of the pinto bean harvest time. Everyone looked forward to harvest, although it was hard work, because they were able to get together with their neighbors and take a break from their hard life for a few hours. During harvest time those living on adjoining farms would arrive to help. The women prepared food and refreshments and at the end of the day, there was often times a dance or a few musicians playing music while neighbors sat around and visited.

Willis described the system of thrashing, "At harvest time the neighbors would pitch in and go from one place to the next thrashing beans." She writes about a time her family was sponsoring the thrashing event and right before lunch the stove blew up blowing soot all over the kitchen and food prepared for the guests already coming up the road.

"What a mess soot all over the fried chicken, light bread and the potato salad. We dusted and blew off all we could," she wrote. "Finally, I just stirred the potato salad and said that maybe they would think it was pepper. None of the men let on if they knew it."

Over twenty years before the establishment of Mountainair a logging community named Eastview had been established by the Spencer and Kayser families along the foothills of the Manzano Mountains. A half century earlier settlers built the town of Manzano to the north. The AT&SF Railroad decided to build the Belen Cutoff and the Spencer Sawmill furnished logs for the railroad ties. Another early community named Monte Alto was located a few miles southwest of Mountainair where a store, cemetery and several buildings were located. The railroad caused Mountainair to boom while Monte Alto was forgotten.

Before the arrival of the railroad, Elisha Dow hauled supplies from Belen and Albuquerque in a covered wagon. He supplied a small store at Eastview as well as the village store near the mountain. The Dow family originally settled at Gran Quivira but later moved to Tajique and established a third store in Chilili. During these years it took three to four days to travel by wagon between Mountainair and Albuquerque. Until 1905 the mail was transported on horseback to Eastview, where W.A. Brown next carried the mail three times a week to Mountainair.

At the height of the pinto bean era over thirty million pounds of pinto beans were shipped from bean elevators in Mountainair each year. As more people homesteaded and the wet years continued the amount of pinto beans tripled between the years of 1916 and 1921. Farms between Mountainair and Claunch produced the most pinto beans and the trains moving the beans were nicknamed the Pinto Bean Express. Claunch and Mountainair both claimed the title of Pinto Bean Capital of the World and between the two towns supplied pinto beans throughout New Mexico and as far away as England during World War II.

All the towns along the railroad tracks had at least one bean elevator. A dry climate in the 1920s closed many elevators as did the drought years of the 1950s. The production of pinto beans slowed in the 1940s when the railroad downsized and another long-term drought hit the state. Most of the pinto bean farmers sought farms elsewhere during the drought but others held on and their family names remain. Many abandoned bean elevators are found throughout the isolated landscape as evidence of a more active past.

The heyday of pinto bean farming was between 1915 and 1930. The Great Depression slowed production and many farms were abandoned or sold to larger ranchers. But the growing of pinto beans increased slightly when the U.S. Government bought beans for food programs during the depression years. The production of pinto beans made its final comeback during World War II when the beans were used as provisions for troops in Europe. Many families ate pinto beans three times a day during the Great Depression.

The small town of Claunch south of Gran Quivira also shared the title of Pinto Bean Capital of the World with Mountainair and a train called the Pinto Bean Express ran between the two towns to transport all the beans.

The community of Claunch was first named DuBois Flats and then Fairview but was eventually named Claunch after L.H. Claunch an early settler and owner of the Claunch Mercantile Store. In the 1890s, Frank DuBois opened the first store and post office in Corona. He would later relocate his family to Claunch and drilled a well. The site initially developed as a camping and watering hole for those traveling between White Oaks, Socorro and Mountainair. Ranchers and pinto bean farmers moved to the area. An updated

Homestead Act granted three hundred and twenty acres to those wanting to homestead what remained of the American frontier.

At Claunch's peak there were five churches, a school, post office, two large grocery stores and mercantile stores, bean elevators and numerous residences. Dances, rodeos, a baseball team and other events provided entertainment for the thriving community. The town had more churches than saloons, and one story tells of L.H. Claunch objecting to the establishment of the Claunch Saloon and the use of his name. The saloon would eventually open though but under a different name.

Singing conventions were popular in Claunch, and for close to twenty years the booming community was considered the Singing Convention Capital of New Mexico. Claunch's first singing convention was held in a brush harbor in 1916 near the town. By the 1940s, singings were held four times a year and homesteaders came from all over the state where they spent the day singing, listening to circuit preachers, eating and visiting with friends and family.

In 1938 the *Mountainair Independent* publicized fried chicken for those attending a singing at Claunch and another quote described the event, "Almost everyone from Gran Quivira went to Claunch to the singing convention on Sunday. All reported a wonderful time and delicious meal."

Mountainair was established as the first incorporated town in Torrance County in 1903. Those instrumental in the incorporation process were J.W. Corbett, E.C. Manning and E.S. Stover all from Kansas. The original town site was 120 acres and originally surveyed by Pitt Ross. The town gained its name from the fresh breezes coming off the nearby Manzano Mountains. The community initially developed as a railroad, farming and ranching community.

W.P. Bartell built the first store in Mountainair and by 1905 the community had started to boom. Dunlavy and McCoy opened a general store, Dr. Black started a drug store, Jim Payne established a barber shop, James Rhoades had a hardware store and Clem Shaffer went into the blacksmith business. The Abo Hotel was located on Broadway Street across from the railroad tracks. Ben Lorey's Hotel originally constructed of wood was destroyed by fire and rebuilt of rock and later renamed the Weaver Hotel.

R.H. Hosher published the first newspaper in town called the *Mountainair Independent*.

Early saloons in Mountainair and elsewhere along the Belen Cutoff did not have an easy time establishing their trade. The AT&SF had trouble with their workers consuming too much alcohol and not returning to work and agreed with town fathers along the route to no whiskey within the town limit. Some saloons were allowed to prosper on the outskirts of town.

Albert Kubena attempted opening the first saloon in Mountainair. He moved to New Mexico from Oklahoma where he had operated a successful saloon business. Those founding the town were determined to not allow the sale of whiskey within the town and soon had an ordinance to that effect. Kubena tried another eating establishment but the business eventually failed and he left town leaving his family behind. Tabet's Bar on the east end of town once provided spirits for those living in Mountainair. The Rosebud Saloon closed in 2010 making it the longest lasting drinking establishment in town.

Mountainair's bean production days were over by the 1940s although a few independent farmers and the Shockey Bean Elevator continued into the 1970s. The Great Depression and dust bowl years that coincided made pinto bean farming next to impossible, and even the pinon and cedar trees died along with the cactus. Sand covered the highways and large dust clouds obscured the view and blanketed anything left uncovered. The old bean fields went into a government program known as Soil Bank where farmers were paid to do nothing to their fields. For another half century the fields were allowed to heal although the old fields are still visible in many areas.

The Farr Bean Elevator is currently used by PNM Signs in Mountainair and has been restored. It remains next to the tracks west of the depot where most of Mountainair's history was written. The Mountainair Railroad Depot remains in use by the BNSF Railroad for storage and office space. Ruins of another bean elevator and boarding house remain on the site, and the train continues to announce its presence as it crosses along the edge of the community.

Pop Shaffer's ghost is said to roam the halls of the Shaffer Hotel in Mountainair. The elevator slides up and down and there is no one in it, items are moved in certain rooms and footsteps are heard in the hall at night but when someone goes to investigate there is no one around. His voice rings out at times in the hotel lobby and even gun shots have been reported. It is well known that Shaffer enjoyed having a drink or two and often returned to the hotel a little intoxicated on certain evenings and a time or two even shot his gun into the ceiling.

He has been described as a wheeler and dealer, a playboy, womanizer, jokester, hotel-keeper, contractor, blacksmith, auto repairman and artist. Reportedly every other word he used was a cuss word and he enjoyed smoking cigars and when not at work he could be found fishing or working on his animal art.

He seemed to have a knack for walking through the woods and finding pieces of wood that resembled an animal and he would shape it into a unique piece of artwork. He built a concrete wall adorned with his rock art still found on the site of his successful business. He often lent money to those settlers coming into the country during the pinto bean era helping them to establish their homesteads and prosper until the drought years persisted and even the mercantile owners in Mountainair were suffering.

He bought a ranch that he named Rancho Bonito a few miles south of Mountainair and spent his later years there working as an artist and creating a small museum. His wooden animals became so popular that tourists arrived from all over the country to see what he had created. In 1940 he traveled to Washington, D.C. where Eleanor Roosevelt helped to arrange an exhibit of his art and it was well attended by the public.

According to most reports, he was not that bad of a guy when he was alive. He was one of the first merchants to set up shop in Mountainair and was instrumental in the early development of the town. He built a blacksmith shop, hotel and drilled a well where people could buy water, in later years he went into the auto repair business and sold farm implements.

His old, hotel remains standing along Mountainair's original main street, but no one has loved the structure quite like Pop did. Maybe that is why his ghost is often heard when someone walks by the building or a shadow is seen passing by a window upstairs. Pop is probably walking the halls checking on the building that was once the center of activity in the early years of Mountainair's history.

Pop Shaffer in front of the Shaffer Hotel. Courtesy: Dorothy Cole Collection.

Mountainair has lost and gained population in the years since and currently has a population of twelve hundred residents. The community traditionally referred to as the "Gateway to Ancient Cities" has become popular for artists and retirees. Travelers along Highway 60 and those recreating in the nearby mountains add to the atmosphere of the railroad town.

4

Willard, Lucy and Pedernal

Willard Depot. Courtesy: Helen Lavell.

Willard was established in 1902 and labeled the Hub of Torrance County. The AT&SF Railroad continued building eastward on the Belen Cutoff and the Santa Fe Central or New Mexico Central Railroad as it was later called moved from Lamy as far as Progresso and Torrance now non-existent towns at the end of the route. The two railroads intersected in Willard making it quite the lively town between 1910 and 1920.

In 1905 Willard had three hotels, a drugstore, W.A. Dunlavy publicized wool, hides and pelts. Guillermo Salas was a wool and pelt merchant and built a large building that housed other businesses as well. There was the Dixie Restaurant and Rooming House, a feed and grain store, the Lutz Mercantile Store and Livery Stable covered most of one whole block where horses, mules, wagons and buggies were sold. Originally, Willard had a much larger business district in its early years as well as the AT&SF depot. The town even had a newspaper called *The Willard Record* published weekly by Eugene Forbes between 1908 and 1932. The town boasted the first bank in Torrance County.

All towns on the frontier had a blacksmith shop. In the town's early years, William Anderson and his son also named William set up the town's first blacksmith shop. They repaired buggies and wagons, sold galvanized tanks, did a little horseshoeing on the side and in later years sold automobiles. The two-story Anderson house stood on the west end of town until the 1960s.

The local barber was George Alter. His barber shop was located in a red brick building on the west side of Becker Street. Later, Alter had a store and café on Highway 60 across the street from one another. Other early settlers in Willard were Epifano Maes and wife Socorro, Cristino Chavez and his wife Carmelita, Marcellino and Marillita Gallegos, Isabel and Rafelita Maes and Saturino Lueras.

One of Willard's oldest and most distinguished settlers was the Hanlon family. Earl Hanlon arrived in New Mexico Territory in 1907 from Waterloo, Iowa where they had worked as morticians. When Hanlon first arrived in town he worked as a bookkeeper for the Willard Mercantile Store. After Earl Hanlon was established in Willard his parents L.C. and Clotilda Hanlon and his three brothers: Frank, Clem and J.H. and two sisters Anna and Maude Hanlon also arrived in town. The family established the Hanlon Mercantile Store and Funeral Home.

Another interesting character who lived in Willard during these years was Dr. Charles Ottosen. He arrived in Willard in 1907 and was soon one of the most influential and important citizens in the growing town. Not only did he practice medicine but he was a builder and constructed many of the early buildings in Willard. He built the Hanlon Mercantile Company and the Ottosen's Drug Store. He was Willard's beloved doctor for over thirty years.

Nate Underwood operated a Willard garage where he sold automobiles during World War I. The Underwood family arrived in Willard from Oklahoma in 1907 and at first tried homesteading southeast of town. Homesteading was not profitable enough for him and the family moved into town and started working for Dr. Ottosen.

Frank Jennings was one of the first lawyers in town. There were rumors at the time that Jennings might have been a bank robber and member of an infamous gang led by his brother Al Jennings who had operated out of Oklahoma a decade earlier. Al and Frank served ten years in federal prison and sought a more peaceful life when they were released.

The Willard Schools opened in 1906 with Miss Mabel Green as its first teacher. Soon the school reached an enrollment of fifty-two students and the school had to hire more teachers. By 1914 the community had a four-room schoolhouse. John Lobb, Sam Hunter and Dr. Ottosen were members of the school board. In the 1920s a high school was built and Thomas Laird of Iowa was the first school superintendent.

Willard was the up and coming community in Torrance County at the turn of the twentieth century. There were more businesses in town than at any other time in its history. There was a motion picture show as early as 1910 and a gasoline pump in town. The pump developed by E.A. Vandevelt pumped gas into a marked glass measure before it went into the car.

The town began to lose population in the 1940s and by 1966 the high school was consolidated with the Estancia Schools. The community currently has a population of two hundred and forty six residents.

Little remains of Lucy the next railroad town east of Willard. In 1915 the community had two general stores, a four-room hotel, blacksmith shop, Justice of the Peace, post office, gas station, and a dozen homes. Lucy had a post office between the years of 1915 and 1942 and the last postmaster was Major Dean.

The people of Lucy loved to sing and often remained after church to sing until the train arrived from the east. Then everyone stopped what they were doing and headed to the depot to watch the train and whoever might be getting on or off. It was a common practice in most railroad communities of the time.

But in 1939 the depot at Lucy was moved to Estancia and used as the depot for the New Mexico Central Branch of the railroad. It now resides on a ranch south of Estancia, a relic of another time and place. To complete Lucy's decline in 2013 the schoolhouse was demolished and the remaining ranch house to the north burned to the ground. Only a scattering of corrals and outbuildings remain where three hundred people once lived.

Church and Sunday school were held in Lucy's schoolhouse. Lucy had a hard time keeping a pastor for their church and a member of the congregation often preached the Sunday sermon. A Methodist preacher was appointed to Mountainair, Willard and Lucy in 1917 and made it to Lucy once or twice a month. Prior to this arrangement, Reverend Ludlow conducted services twice a month and a Baptist minister once a month.

The cemetery also stands. In 2013, former residents and the land's owner fenced the cemetery, whose graves and tombstones were nearly destroyed by grazing cattle. A gate and list of those buried have been added at the entrance. It is all that survives of Lucy.

The small community of Lucy had a civic mind in its early years. The Ladies Aid Society bought a house and had it moved to Lucy to use for their meetings. The house was later used as a Red Cross building and then rented to one of the teachers at the school.

The town was originally named Lucia, but the name later changed to Lucy and was named after one of three women related to railroad men pioneering the Belen Cutoff. It was either named after the wife of James Dunn the chief engineer, after a railroad attorney's mother or possibly after Lucy Meyers the daughter of Frank Meyers the construction engineer for the AT&SF. It is possible it was named after all three women.

The Lucy School was in session between 1919 and 1940. Residents of the community during the early years were the families of Austin, Baker and McGillivray. A Mrs. Klaunch managed and lived in the hotel. The social center for the small railroad community was the first schoolhouse. Debates, talks on various subjects and group singings were popular activities during these years.

Children attending school in Lucy and throughout the New Mexico frontier were transported in a Ford truck with a canvas top with seats running along the sides. Thirty kids usually rode in this type of bus and many of the children were on the bus seven to eight hours a day.

Roy Cline established his roadside business at Lucy before moving to Clines Corners. The Cline family moved to New Mexico from Arkansas in 1926. They tried farming near Moriarty but ended up trading the farm for a small hotel when the farm failed to produce. The hotel business was not much better and Cline soon moved again. This time they tried a service station at Lucy with a hamburger joint on the side, but most businesses during the Great Depression were not successful.

The family soon left Lucy and moved closer to what would become Route 66. Cline took his service station down in pieces and convinced a wildcat bean hauler to transport it to his new location. When the Cline family moved to this site Route 66 was only seven years old. The highway was unpaved with few gas stations and eating places along the route.

One of the reasons Roy Cline's roadside business succeeded was he enjoyed visiting more than working and kept his visitors enthralled with stories and tall tales. One of his favorite past-times was sitting in the shade reading Wild West magazines and smoking Prince Albert cigars while one of his six daughters ran the filling station. He yelled at them to wait on that car when someone arrived. He also gave away free Conoco maps.

With the drought and depression years, the majority of Lucy's residents could not make a living. Some abandoned their homesteads while others sold out to cattle and sheep ranchers. The cemetery provides the names of those who once lived in the present-day ghost town. It is hard to imagine Lucy during its heyday, as even most of the foundations of the buildings once serving as the town are gone. Many of the homes of the homesteaders were placed directly on the ground or rocks were used as foundations and time has even erased their locations.

Abandoned buildings scattered along the railroad tracks a few miles south of Highway 60 mark the location of the former railroad town of Pedernal. The community was founded in 1902 and named for the Pedernal Hills to the north. The name pedernal is a Spanish word meaning flint or flinty, and the town boomed for twenty years because of the railroad and bean elevators it supplied in the Estancia Valley. J.C. Shelton and his wife ran the depot, telegraph office and a store near the tracks and Mrs. Shelton served as the first postmistress.

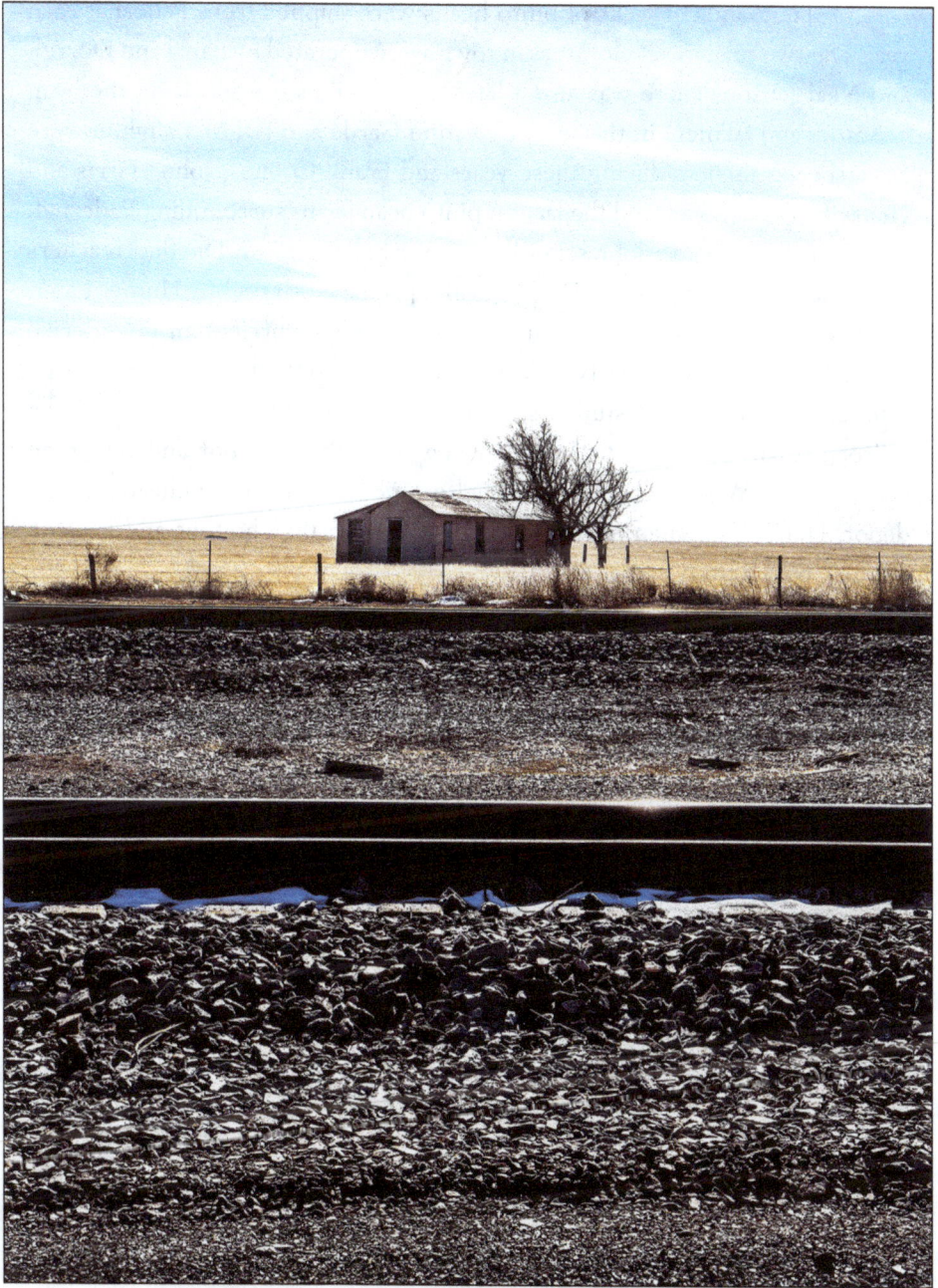

Pedernal. Courtesy: Marilyn Conway Photography.

Thousands of sacks of pinto beans were shipped from Pedernal each year. The two main bean elevators in town were operated by Baird and Dorrell and Neal Jenson. There was also a large mercantile store servicing the bean elevators and farmers in the area. Celestino Garde and Ted McLaughlin were large sheep ranchers during these years and Frank Coones, John Harris and Henry Eshleman operated the largest pinto bean farms surrounding Pedernal.

A four-room adobe schoolhouse was built in 1935. The first teachers were Marie Lamb and Ruth Dean and the principal Mrs. C.C. Hume. Later, the first two years of high school were added to the curriculum in Pedernal but at the end of the first two years, the high school students were bussed into Encino for lack of students. Soon, the few students remaining in the railroad town were sent to Encino when the railroad depot and telegraph office closed. When Mr. and Mrs. Shelton moved due to the closure of the depot, Henry Eshleman purchased the store from the Sheltons and became the new postmaster.

More survives intact of Pedernal than other ghost towns along the track but overgrown weeds and a fence bars visitors from the site. Ruins of homes and businesses remain showing the layout of many railroad towns along the route. The train passes to the south as a reminder of the town's railroad past.

5

Negra and Encino

Gas Station at Negra. Courtesy: Marilyn Conway Photography.

Few facts remain about the people and events making up the history of the small, farming community of Negra. A vintage gas station and old tourist court stand near Highway 60 as proof of its existence. The main part of the town was across the railroad tracks to the south. C.E. Davenport, the first postmaster of Encino originally constructed and operated the business. Negra's post office was established in 1909 but had closed by 1918.

Water was often a problem along the railroad route but not so in Negra. The town had more water than it could use and several of its residents went into the water hauling business. Water was hauled to Encino, Clines Corners, Duran, Vaughn and anywhere else it was needed in the area.

The red rock house and out buildings of homesteaders Ollie and Hallie Williams are on the east side of the road. An old house, piles of wood and an overgrown cemetery are all that remain of the once booming town of Negra. Negra's main street consisted of the red-brick home of the Williams' family on the east side of the road. On the west side was located a teacher's house, one-room schoolhouse and a couple other structures.

Hallie and Carrie Walker arrived in Negra to homestead and teach in the one-room schoolhouse. They both had degrees from Baylor University in Texas and had taught before arriving in Negra. Hallie would eventually marry another homesteader named Ollie Williams, who operated the gas station and tourist court at Negra before starting his mercantile business in Encino.

Campgrounds referred to as tourist courts were popular the first fifty years of the twentieth century. These early businesses consisted of small cabins and areas to camp. Some even provided corrals for livestock. Showers were available at a few campgrounds, and almost all provided residents with buckets of water for cooking and cleaning.

During World War II when there was a shortage of male teachers in the United States, Hallie taught math at Encino High School. Between the years of 1939 and 1942, she painted four murals on the walls of Encino's gymnasium. She was commissioned $20.00 a mural by the senior classes of those years. Unfortunately, the murals have since been destroyed.

Encino, meaning oak in Spanish, was named for the low, oak brush once covering the land between the Pedernal Hills and Duran Mesa. Before 1900, those traveling New Mexico's eastern plains often stopped at a spring near present-day Encino where a fortress-like structure was built for those needing accommodations. During New Mexico's territorial days, there were few camping spots with a reliable water source between Roswell, Santa Fe and Las Vegas the main towns of commerce on New Mexico's east side.

Jewel Dunn and Jim McLaughlin, Encino 1949. Courtesy: June McLaughlin.

Bonnie Salas homesteaded the town site of Encino, and both sheep and cattle ranchers settled on the endless plains surrounding the town. Mariano Mondosa had forty thousand head of sheep at one time. F.H. Wood, the Duran family, the Tenorios, Victor Perez and Jesus Abeyta are a few of the original ranchers settling near Encino. The ranch of Jacob Ysarri was often used as a resting place for wagons pulled by oxen in the early years.

Victor Perez immigrated to the United States from Isaba, Spain in 1904 when he was fifteen years old. After landing in New York harbor, he traveled by train to Lamy near Santa Fe and then on by wagon to Vaughn and Encino where a Basque community had developed. Many of the same families from Spain settled along the railroad tracks as the town of Encino was founded.

Perez would become one of the pioneer ranchers in the area and his family contributed much to the settlement and early development of Encino. His son Ernest Perez served as the President of the Encino School Board for thirty-five years and was a member of the New Mexico Cattle Growers Association and the National Sheep Industry Association.

Victor Perez settled on land between Encino and Clines Corners and raised a family, as well as Rambouillet sheep and registered Hereford cattle. Perez' original ranch would eventually be divided three ways among his children and his descendants continue operating the ranch today. Perez tried to help local kids during the depression years by hiring them to help with ranching but most of the population had moved away or were fighting in World War II.

When Perez first settled on his ranch wolves caused problems for those raising cattle and especially sheep. One way early ranchers dealt with the problem was by killing burros and leaving strychnine inside for the wolves to eat. The Perez family also used llamas to protect the sheep.

Encino's heyday was during the 1930s. Most of the population lived in dugouts surrounding the town and electricity was provided within the town limits by a private electricity provider who ran a generator when the town needed lights. The electric co-op would not arrive until the late 1940s. Most of those settling the area used wind chargers or kerosene for lamps.

Encino had a post office by 1907 and the first mercantile store in town was built by B.G. Bond & Brothers in 1905. In the early years Encino had two newspapers and two medical doctors. One newspaper was named the *Encino Progress* and the other the *Encino Enterprise*. The *Encino Enterprise* would continue with publication until the 1920s and the last editor was E.L. Hinton. By 1908 both a Dr. Michaels and a Dr. Miller had set up medical practices in town. With the construction of the railroad depot Encino experienced a minor boom for a few decades before losing population.

The Bond brothers had the only store in town until 1908 when A.R. Cecil established a lumber business. When the railroad decided they needed a depot in Encino, the Bond brothers bought forty acres from Bonnie Salas and sold it to the railroad company.

The first agent at the newly finished depot was a Mr. Bishop, and while the depot was completed he had an office in the Bond Mercantile Store. The last agent of the Encino Depot was Howard Sims. The main business district of the town spread out along the tracks and catered to ranchers, farmers, travelers and the railroad company.

Albert and Hallie Williams opened the second mercantile store in Encino located on Railroad Street. When Highway 60 was routed through the community, it became the main street and the businesses along Railroad Street either moved or died. The Williams moved their store and gas station to a location along Highway 60. The original Williams Store was said to have a somewhat smelly buffalo head above the cash register and was a common place for members of the community to hang out when in town.

R.C. Dillon was one of Encino's early pioneers, and he worked hard to draw attention to the small community. After serving in the senate, he was elected the eighth governor of New Mexico and served two terms starting in 1927. Dillon was born in St. Louis, Missouri in 1877 and when he was twelve years old moved with his family to Springer in northern New Mexico. He worked as the manager of the B.G. Bond Mercantile before opening his own store in 1938 naming it R.C. Dillon & Company. The building is still along Railroad Street with his fading name on the outside.

Dillon appears to have been a well-liked governor and one of the first Republicans elected to a second term. He worked on paving, improving and creating roads in rural areas of the state. Dillon had some political clout as political figures throughout the state often stopped by his house in Encino where he threw elaborate dinner parties. He was instrumental in the establishment of Eastern New Mexico University in Portales. Dillon thought higher education a key to the future of the state especially for those living in rural areas where an education was not always available.

Roads do not seem like a big deal today, but Highway 60 would not be completely paved until the 1950s. There were many small motels and tourist courts along the route to provide for those traveling the often muddy, bumpy, primitive roads of the era. These early travelers carried additional tires plus camping gear, food and water as the roads were as unreliable as the vehicles of the era. Dillon pushed for more road construction projects and better rest areas for highway travelers. When Dillon took office in the 1920s many people living in isolated areas of New Mexico traveled by horse and buggy or on horseback and in most cases made a lot better time.

Encino's decline began in 1965 with the closing of the railroad depot, and by 1982 the high school was consolidated with the schools in Vaughn. The brick elementary school now houses the offices of the Village of Encino and town library. The adobe, high school and gymnasium erected by the WPA between 1936 and 1939 were torn down in 2013 due to safety issues. The old gymnasium where the Bean Valley Tournament was once played and couples danced to their high school prom has disappeared as has happened to most of the residences in the small town.

The removal of the railroad depot and the closure of the school system in Encino have added much to its demise. With their removal went the heart of the town. The people soon followed, leaving nothing but abandoned buildings and years of memories behind. The population of Encino in the 2010 census was sixty-four residents.

Encino Depot 1948. Courtesy: June McLaughlin.

6

Vaughn, Las Chavez Harvey House and Cedar Street

Vaughn was named for Major G.W. Vaughn a civil engineer for the AT&SF Railroad. Before the railroad boosted the town's population, the location was a resting place for large cattle herds traveling the Stinson Cattle Trail from Texas. Jim Stinson, an employee of the New Mexico Land & Livestock Company drove twenty thousand head of cattle to the Estancia Valley where they were sold to settlers and helped to supply western forts in 1882.

The Southern Pacific was the first to arrive in Vaughn and a small community soon developed. Vaughn was a rough town in its early days with cowboys traveling the Stinson Cattle Trail and outlaws using the area for their own gain. The cattle town was full of brothels and saloons and controlled by a rough element of railroad men and those living on the edge of the law. The original town site near the Stinson Cattle Trail was called Vaughn.

Six years later in 1905 the AT&SF intersected with the Southern Pacific line. The Santa Fe Railroad decided to make Vaughn a division point, and this caused tension between the two railroad companies. In the beginning, the AT&SF tried to buy out the Southern Pacific, but that did not work because they wanted too much money. So, the AT&SF formed their own community one mile east of Vaughn and named their new town East Vaughn. Later, the two areas were referred to as Old Town and New Town. The towns had two separate post offices but eventually the children would attend the same school. The two towns later merged and used the name Vaughn.

The *Carlsbad Current* left behind a description of early Vaughn in 1908, "The so called town of Vaughn is about a mile and a half west of the depot. The Santa Fe Company it is said will build a town at the depot and endeavor to kill off the town of Vaughn where water is sold for sixty cents a barrel and where the nearest well is fifty miles away."

From the beginning Vaughn had problems with water, and in 1908 the AT&SF built two underground cisterns and a steel water tank was installed. Water was hauled in tank cars from Willard and Negra. The Southern Pacific used a wooden pipe that came all the way from Bonito Lake a hundred miles to the south, and the AT&SF made a deal with the Southern Pacific to siphon water off their pipe for twenty four cents every thousand gallons. This water was used for steaming engines and in the repair shops.

Vaughn was an active town during its infancy and into the 1950s. A division point was generally established every one hundred miles and had a larger yard with multiple tracks and a roundhouse for train maintenance plus a railroad office. Division points were always busy places with trains coming and going, crews often changed at the division points and lived in the area. Also there were three highways coming in and out of Vaughn making it quite the place during its heyday years. Major division points in New Mexico were Albuquerque, Chama, Clovis, Raton, Gallup and Vaughn.

The Los Chavez Harvey House was erected in Vaughn in 1910 and named after the Chavez family, one of the original Spanish settlers arriving with Don Juan de Onate in 1598. The Los Chavez was a training center for new, inexperienced Harvey Girls. They were taught the correct way to treat customers and keep their uniforms spotless during an entire shift. The hotel had few overnight guests and reserved a few rooms for teachers at the nearby school. In the book *Harvey Girls: Women Who Opened the West* by Lesley Poling-Kempes, a Harvey Girl named Alice Garnas described Vaughn in 1926, "Vaughn was a shocking place. There was no place to go, nothing to do. Just Vaughn and those wide plains on all sides—cattle country, but it was for me."

Charles Lindbergh was forced to land near Vaughn in 1928 because of engine failure. He was stranded in town for a couple of days while waiting on a part and stayed at the Harvey House. The Harvey Girls all wanted a glimpse of the famous pilot, but he was not overly interested in striking up a conversation or interacting with the girls.

While on a fishing trip, Will Rogers and a group of friends had to make an unscheduled landing in Vaughn due to bad weather in 1935. They spent the night at the Harvey House and entertained the guests. Rogers even filed one of his newspaper columns from Vaughn making fun of the event.

Vaughn's Harvey House was the center of the community. Everyone ate at the restaurant and socialized and drank while there. The busboys rang a small bell when the first passengers stepped down from the train so their meals were ready when they reached the dining room. Those not riding the train were also served with quick, professional service.

According to Vaughn native Paul Strong, "East Vaughn developed when the Santa Fe built a depot, Harvey House, reading room, coal chute and roundhouse where the cars were cleaned and serviced," pointed out Strong. "The Harvey House and the train depot were on the north side of the road, and the rest of the town was built on the south side."

"I was only a kid in 1939 but I remember when the Harvey House was knocked down and razed by the railroad," stated Strong. "The building was not used for over twenty years and in the late 1960s the railroad decided to tear it down. Since the structure was mostly made of concrete, the railroad knocked it down."

Charlie Panebouef, also from Vaughn, remembers the old, Harvey House, "The story goes that the railroad left everything on the tables, silverware and china and so forth and boarded up the building as soon as it closed," he explained. "Of course all the kids wanted to get in there and see what was inside but the railroad had it so secure it was impossible to trespass."

In the late 1960s the railroad demolished the building. "They came in trucks and boxed up and removed everything from the inside," Panebouef explained. "Then they tore the building down and removed the debris."

Vaughn's first main street was Cedar Street and the original route of Highway 60 through town. An important business on Cedar Street during this era was the Panebouef Bar. The proprietor Carlos Panebouef was a "behind the scene" politician and promoter of the town. Ranchers, politicians and those running the state often stopped at the bar where important decisions were made over drinks and a game of pool.

During the depression years Carlos Panebouef prepared and distributed boxes of food to the community. "In many cases if it had not been for Carlos' generosity, the people of Vaughn would have starved. He made up boxes of food for the children, especially at Christmas time and made sure everyone at least had beans to eat and a jar of Rex Jelly," stated Charlie Panebouef. "He also sold old ewes for three to five dollars each to those who could not afford food."

Cedar Street in Vaughn. Courtesy: Marilyn Conway Photography.

The train once stopped at the end of Cedar Street across the tracks on the north side where the Las Tusas Bar & Brothel was located. "My granddad told me stories about the brothel when I was a kid. The train would stop there along its route and those aboard would get off and grab something to drink and fulfill their other vices before moving on," explained Panebouef.

The brothel was blown up in the 1920s. "Several of the wives in Vaughn got tired of their husbands frequenting the establishment and had it blown up," stated Panebouef. "I cannot remember the name of the brothel owner but the story goes that he found husbands for all the girls who had been working for him before leaving town."

During prohibition, Carlos Panebouef operated underground slot machines in Vaughn, Corona, Duran, Carrizozo and Capitan. According to Charlie Panebouef the machines were built into a cabinet that locked into the wall when they needed to be hidden. The slot machines were buried in a secret location in Vaughn and later dug up and sold by family members.

An interesting character living in Vaughn during the depression years was referred to as the Vagabond Artist. No one remembers his true identity anymore, but he painted several murals on the walls of a bar on Cedar Street and other murals throughout the town. He mainly worked for room, board and his drinks but left behind exceptional murals for the townspeople to enjoy.

Vaughn had many more businesses along its Main Street than today and had at least five bars, a Chevrolet Agency, Ford Dealership, Drive in Restaurant, Ranch House Café & Corral Bar, the Vaughn Hotel & Restaurant, a drug store, Hodges Filling Station and a elementary school and high school although the original elementary school was burned down by a student who had been expelled but was rebuilt a few years later.

Vaughn was incorporated in 1919 and had a population of nine hundred residents by 1920. Ranching and the railroad remains an important part of the town's economy. In the 2010 census Vaughn had a population of four hundred and thirty seven people, yet the community remains an important crossroads on New Mexico's eastern plains.

7

Yeso, Fort Sumner and Billy the Kid

After leaving Vaughn, the route flattens as the highway traverses the landscape of New Mexico's eastern plains on its way to Yeso, Fort Sumner and the Pecos River. The next vanishing community on the route is Yeso, located between Vaughn and Fort Sumner and once an active, little community where the train stopped for the benefit of the ranchers in the area.

Yeso was founded in 1906 and named for the nearby Yeso Creek. Yeso is a Spanish word meaning gypsum as there are large deposits in the area. One of the first frame depots was built at Yeso and it was one of the last to close along the route in 1968.

Old foundations and abandoned buildings suggest Yeso was once a larger community with more businesses and people than today. One building has the name Hotel Mesa painted on one side and Museum, Guns & Antiques on another. A dusty sign near the door advertises the Good Vibes Café serving tea and lunch.

The Overland Mercantile Store is spelled out on the wall of a nearby building. Across the highway on the south side is a full-service filling station built in the style of the 1920s when cars traveled dirt roads as they crossed New Mexico on their way to either coast.

A school was built by the WPA in 1940 and closed in 1966 shortly before the railroad depot was closed. Yeso had a population of two hundred and thirty nine in 1940 and ten years later it had actually grown to three hundred and fifty residents. Although, Yeso is considered a ghost town a few families still remain in town.

After Yeso was founded it became a trading center for ranchers and farmers. The railroad depot helped to keep the town alive and was a favorite location for those residing in the small community. Yeso had one of the best baseball teams in eastern New Mexico. The baseball craze was sweeping the country and every small town had at least one team. Members of the winning team were: N. O'Connor was pitcher, Francis played on third, Reynolds served as short stop, another O'Connor was on first base, A. Taylor was the catcher and sometimes pitcher, D. Hutchison played right field, E. Hutchison played second base and Kendrick played right field. Baseball games were normally scheduled for Sunday and the entire town attended.

According to F. Stanley in the *Yeso, New Mexico Story,* "It was unfortunate that the town was settled at a time New Mexico was going through one of the droughts in her history. Like all end of the track towns when the railroad was rebuilding Yeso had its rough element, its hard-drinking, hard shooting, hard fighting characters but once the gangs moved along eastward Yeso settled back to become an important community."

A.A. Ryan was the owner of the Yeso town site and encouraged settlement of the community. In the beginning Yeso kept up with the other towns in population and growth. Yeso had a post office by 1909 with the name spelled Yesso. It was closed a few months later and reopened as Yeso. William S. Moore was the first postmaster under both names. Yeso began its history in Guadalupe County but was later transferred to De Baca County.

Fort Sumner is most famous as the site where Billy the Kid is buried in the old military cemetery with his two friends and outlaw partners Charlie Bowdre and Tom O'Folliard. The three friends share one tombstone with the word Pals chiseled at the top.

Fort Sumner's history began in 1862 when congress authorized the establishment of a military fort and Indian Reservation. The fort was named for General Edwin Vose Sumner who passed away during its construction. An Indian reservation named Bosque Redondo was established for Mescalero Apache and Navajo Indians near the fort. By the summer of 1863 four hundred Mescalero families had moved to the site.

The fort was abandoned in 1868 after the government admitted their reservation experiment had been a mistake and the tribes were allowed to return to their homeland. Lucien Maxwell bought the fort and surrounding land for five thousand dollars. The community surrounding the Maxwell land was called Fort Sumner and was a lawless area during its early years often attracting outlaws, cattle rustlers and other shady characters. Lucien turned over the operation of the ranch to his son Pete Maxwell a friend of the outlaw Billy the Kid.

Due to its isolation and lack of law enforcement, Fort Sumner was often used as the headquarters of cattle rustlers. The Mexican people making up the town's population were friends with Billy the Kid and his gang. His right-hand man Charlie Bowdre married a woman from the community. The people of Fort Sumner often protected the outlaws and gave them food and supplies when they were hiding from a posse. Billy the Kid felt safe and at home in Fort Sumner and often returned to the location when needing rest and a place to hide.

Billy was killed in Pete Maxwell's bedroom by Lincoln County Sheriff Pat Garrett in 1881. There are different versions to the story as to why the Kid was on Maxwell's porch in the first place. But, Garrett recognized his voice and shot in the dark killing Billy the Kid. Friends mourned the death of the outlaw and prepared his body for burial. The Maxwell family sold the old fort in 1884.

- - - -

The AT&SF laid out the town site of Sunnyside seven miles to the northwest of the fort in 1905. The site was initially a construction camp where the railroad planned on building a bridge across the Pecos River, probably one of their more difficult construction projects along the route. Sunnyside also developed as a rowdy frontier town along the tracks with more saloons and bordellos than other businesses. Two of the first establishments in town were the Blue Goose and Dog Bars.

At first the towns of Fort Sumner and Sunnyside co-existed with Fort Sumner Avenue now Highway 60 as the dividing line. The depot served both communities. When the station was built passenger trains from the west saw the words Sunnyside on the end of the depot and those from the east Fort Sumner.

In the summer of 1908 most of the area was destroyed by a tornado. Women and children were sent to the train depot for safety because of the building's sturdy construction. Re-building after the tornado was financially hard on both towns and they decided to pool their resources and voted to become one town under the name of Fort Sumner in 1909.

Oliver Loving and Charles Goodnight were the first Texans to trail herds of cattle to Colorado and Montana establishing the Goodnight-Loving Trail. Loving was killed by Comanche near present-day Fort Sumner and remained in a shallow grave until the following spring when Goodnight exhumed the body and took it back to Texas. The story of the two men was portrayed in the book and movie *Lonesome Dove* by McMurtry.

Fort Sumner was originally in San Miguel County but became the county seat of De Baca County in 1917 and has since maintained a population between fifteen hundred and two thousand residents. Fort Sumner's main economy is ranching, farming and tourism. The impressive De Baca County Courthouse, built in 1930, was listed on the National Register of Historic Places in 1987.

De Baca County Courthouse. Author's collection.

The Fort Sumner Municipal Airport has an interesting past. In the 1920s the Transcontinental Air Transport Airline built an airfield near Fort Sumner. The airline planned on expanding transcontinental travel but had to stop during the Great Depression when there was no funding for the project. The airfield was re-opened by the Army Air Corp during World War II and used as a training base for pilots.

The site of Billy the Kid's grave and the history of the old fort attracts visitors as well as the Billy the Kid Museum and original railroad depot along the tracks. Nearby Fort Sumner Lake provides recreational opportunities as the site is a popular destination for fishing and boating.

8

Taiban, Tolar and Melrose

The next town stacked out by the AT&SF Railroad was Taiban named for the nearby creek. In its earlier history the creek was referred to as Brazil Creek for a Portuguese immigrant arriving in the area in 1871. No one seems to know the real meaning of the word Taiban, but one surviving story explains it as a Comanche word meaning horsetail which relates to the tributaries of the creek.

The ladies of Taiban had ice cream socials, box suppers and other events in an attempt to raise money for the schoolhouse constructed in 1906. Businessmen soon arrived at the location and a Dr. Darbeson built a drug store, W.B. Hill bought part of the town site, and the Wilson brothers bought him out. Hill had a store selling notions and shoes.

To have or not have a saloon caused problems in the early years of Taiban's history. The Pink Pony Saloon & Dancehall attracted a drinking and partying element to the community that was not appreciated by everyone. Roosevelt County to the east was a dry county (no alcohol sales) in fact there were many dry counties eastward in Texas and Oklahoma. During prohibition out of county and out of state cars arrived at the Pink Pony often. The bar advertised cock fighting and a live snake den in the basement.

Taiban actually had its own airport during these years and the wealthy flew in from adjoining states and counties to purchase alcohol. Taiban was known as the Bootlegging Capital of Eastern New Mexico and West Texas. By 1960 the Pink Pony was one of the only businesses still in operation in the small community. Another drinking establishment on the same street during these years was Mac's Bar and bootleggers would arrive from the east, pick up alcohol and leave before they were caught.

Another element in the small town was the well to do church goers. In the fall of 1908 they began construction on the Presbyterian Church still standing in the small community. The church was built for two hundred and fifty dollars but the Presbyterian women only had raised a hundred dollars and had to borrow from the Baptist congregation and the Taiban Savings Bank.

The church would eventually have a baby grand piano, pot-bellied stove and bell tower. The church building was used for weddings, funerals, family reunions, box suppers and more. Although, the town had a religious element, the sale of alcohol is what kept the town going through the Great Depression when other businesses were closing.

In December of 1880 Billy the Kid, Tom O'Folliard, Charlie Bowdre and others caused problems in the gold mining town of White Oaks north of Carrizozo. A posse chased the group to the Great House Stage Stop and Tavern south of Corona. A standoff between the two groups occurred and Deputy James Carlyle went inside to try and parley with the group. Instead of talking to Carlyle the outlaws took him prisoner. The posse threatened that if Carlyle was not immediately released a hostage would be shot.

A member of the posse fired a shot and Carlyle thought the posse was starting to kill hostages and jumped out the window of the stage stop. Gunfire erupted between the two groups and Carlyle was killed. The gunmen escaped and it has never been proved who really killed Carlyle as those outside thought he was one of the outlaws trying to escape.

Billy the Kid's group took off for Fort Sumner. In the meantime Pat Garrett had organized a posse and was waiting in the old hospital near Charlie Bowdre's house in Fort Sumner for them to return. The group rode into town single file, tired after their long ride across the country and were looking forward to relaxing by the fire for the evening.

Garrett yelled for the group to surrender but they scattered in all directions. Garret shot and killed Tom O'Folliard when he tried to aim his gun. The gang headed for Stinking Springs a rock house near Taiban used by sheepherders and those needing a place to camp. By three o'clock in the morning Garrett and his posse had the rock house surrounded. Shortly before dawn, Charlie Bowdre came out of the building to take care of the horses and Garrett shot and killed him thinking he was Billy. All day long casual firing and yelling back and forth between the two groups took place. Garrett started cooking and making coffee for the posse, and the Kid and his gang succumbed to the smell of food and decided to surrender.

The group rode back to Fort Sumner on Christmas day and took the body of Charlie Bowdre to his widow's house before continuing to Las Vegas and eventually Santa Fe where the Kid spent two months in jail. Later, he was transported to Mesilla south of Las Cruces where he was tried and found guilty of the killing of Sheriff Brady in Lincoln. He was sentenced to hang until dead on a gallows in Lincoln.

Tolar, located eighteen miles west of Melrose had every reason to boom in 1911 when the town was founded. There were six hundred people living in the booming community and talk of oil attracted cattlemen and homesteaders to the area. Tolar was established as a location along the proposed Belen Cutoff to supply sand and gravel to prepare the road bed for the railroad tracks.

The Tolar post office was in operation between the years of 1905 and 1946. The first postmaster was J.W. Coleman and he is responsible for naming the town Tolar after a town in Texas where he had lived before relocating to New Mexico. Jason Little published the first newspaper in town called the *Tolar Tribune* in 1908.

J.W. Coleman was the father of Tolar and was instrumental in the early growth and notice of the town. The town soon attracted settlers and vied for the division point, as did all the small towns on the route. According to F. Stanley in the *Tolar, New Mexico Story,* "There is a large work force on the big cut near J.W. Coleman's store. They have two traction engines and about forty teams. The indications are that we will have a town at or near this place. It is hoped we get the division point."

The first residents of Tolar were sure the town would become a division point and built a large fairground, baseball diamond, a grandstand and a half mile circular race track. Later, they would use the facilities for games and races on Sundays, holidays and especially the Fourth of July. The most important baseball game was always the one with Taiban.

The town came close to being washed away in a flood soon after it was established but was able to rebuild. Stanley wrote about the occurrence, "Almocha Draw had lots of water that has spread over an area one half mile wide. Walter Morris and Mr. Honey, who have S.F. Wooding's slaughter pens, lost everything they had the water came down too quick for them to save anything. They abandoned the houses and went to higher ground as the adobe walls at Mr. Seter's house crumbed in, and Mr. Tyson suffered considerable damage."

In March of 1933 the AT&SF closed Tolar's railroad depot and the decline of the town began. In November of 1944 a passing munitions train exploded and leveled the town. Tremors from the blast were felt in Melrose, Fort Sumner and Portales and as far away as Hereford, Texas. Another newspaper reported that the dishes on people's tables rattled in Farwell, Texas and a vehicle on the nearby highway had all four tires blown off.

A train consisting of eighty one cars was traveling west from Clovis when a crew member detected a hot box under a fuel oil tanker car. The engineer was slowing down near Tolar to check the problem when the fuel oil tanker broke off, jumped the track taking thirty six cars with it and exploded. The fire was unstoppable as it spread through the dry, wooden boxcars before anyone had time to stop it.

Also connected to the train was a car containing forty seven tons of high explosives en route to help with the war in Europe. When the fire reached the car the explosives debris shot high into the air, breaking out windows and caving in the roofs of the houses closest to the track.

Almost every house or building in town was either damaged or destroyed but only one resident was killed. Jess Brown was killed when a piece of metal hit him in the head and twenty others wounded. J.A. Watkins received severe head injuries, and Mrs. Homer and A.C. Larsh were thrown to the ground near the post office although not seriously hurt. The Watkins Mercantile, Smith's Grocery and post office were destroyed.

Fortunately, only thirty or so residents were in town when the explosion occurred. Most were at work or running errands and the children were attending school in Taiban. The explosion and train derailment left a crater twenty feet long and sixty feet wide across downtown Tolar. Most of the residents of Tolar moved to Melrose or Fort Sumner and the town began its final decline.

Many of the residents thought the Japanese had attacked or somehow sabotaged the train. A major blizzard also caused problems for the residents of Tolar and the town never recovered from the explosion and little evidence remains of the town's former glory.

Train near Melrose. Author's collection.

Melrose, initially established as a division point along the Belen Cutoff was laid out by the AT&SF in 1906 and named for Melrose, Ohio. The town originally called Brownhorn after Walter "Wildhorse" Brown and Lonny Horn owner of the Pig Pen Ranch was originally located where the ranches of the two men bordered and a small settlement developed in 1882 before the arrival of the railroad. The Pig Pen Ranch is the oldest ranch in Curry County established in 1881.

The AT&SF intended using Melrose for a division point and had the depot completed and walls up to the windowsills on the roundhouse when they changed their minds and made Clovis the division point instead. Melrose had water problems from the start and inflated land prices made it unfeasible as the division point.

J.L. Downing is considered the father of Melrose. He was born in Virginia but moved to Missouri where he became involved in real estate. He worked for the good of the community and encouraged homesteaders to settle the vast, eastern plains of the state. When the town ran out of water he gave free water from his own well until settlers could dig their own.

L.D. Beckworth started the first newspaper in 1902 but after a few issues it was discontinued until 1909. An amazing number of newspapers tried making a go in the young town, but only the *Melrose Democrat, Melrose Index* and the *Melrose Highlight-Enterprise* made lasting contributions to the community.

Most of the town was destroyed by fire in 1914. Fifteen buildings were destroyed including the town's business district. Melrose as most frontier towns was plagued by fire. Another fire in 1917 burned the Turner Store, Masonic Lodge, Dr. Lynch's office, the post office, meat market and Mack's Pool Hall.

In the beginning the Presbyterian Church served as the school but as early as 1908 the town had a four-room schoolhouse and four teachers. An even larger school was built between 1909 and 1910. When the old school was torn down much of the lumber and materials were used on the new one, and the same was done again in 1917 when an even larger school was needed.

In the 1940s the Melrose Women's Club presented numerous plays in the school auditorium. The plays were well received by the community. The local newspaper congratulated the group on bringing entertainment and culture to the town. The most popular play was titled *Flapper Grandma*.

Early communities on the American frontier provided many opportunities for its citizens to get together. There were political meetings, plays, literary meetings, baseball and basketball games, dances, church camp meetings, singings and women's clubs. Women's clubs provided quilting bees, crafting and scrapbooking opportunities with pot luck and music.

Melrose has dropped in population since the days of its initial division point status, and the railroad depot stands abandoned near the tracks with grain silos in the background. The population of the community is currently seven hundred and fifty one residents and the economy relies on farming and ranching.

9

Clovis and Texico

Harvey House and Grounds.   Clovis, N. M.

Clovis Harvey House and Grounds. Author's collection.

Clovis established in 1906 was originally called Riley's Switch. There are conflicting stories as to the origin of the Riley name, but the town site changed its name to Clovis in 1907. Most accounts agree the community was named after Clovis the first Christian King of France. Clovis developed as a railroad, ranching and farming community and was incorporated in 1909. Clayton Reed and C. V. Steed started the first business in town in real estate.

There was much speculation in the beginning as to where the railroad would place the division point. The AT&SF purchased four hundred acres at Clovis at a price of twelve thousand dollars and started drilling water wells.

When a good supply of water was found, the railroad tore up the new roadbed from Texico to Portales on the Pecos Valley Line sealing their decision to make Clovis the division point.

All the towns along the proposed Belen Cutoff vied to become a division point. On the Fourth of July in 1908 a gang of railroad workers from the Pecos Valley Railroad Company took a company of three hundred men and started to tear up the track since they planned on rerouting all trains through the Cameo Cutoff to Clovis.

When the people of Texico heard what the railroad men were doing they organized a body of one hundred and sixty men to stop the workers from proceeding. Luckily, no one was hurt because of the quick action of Avery Turner, the general manager for the company. He ordered the trackmen to stop work until the matter could be peacefully resolved.

Afterwards the AT&SF began construction on the depot, Gran Quivira Harvey House, a reading room, administrative offices and a railroad hospital nearby. A machine shop, storehouse and roadhouse were built and by 1915 a Railroad Express Agency building was constructed west of the railroad depot.

The Gran Quivira was named after the Spanish mission and Tompiro pueblo near Mountainair now part of Salinas Pueblo Missions National Monument. The Harvey House was the first hotel in Clovis to have a banquet room. The manager of the hotel John Prichard marketed the hotel as a place for residents and tourists to stop and enjoy a good meal and communication with others.

Cannon Air Force Base is another major employer and economic boost to the community. A private passenger facility named Portair Field was established on the site in the 1920s. Charles Lindbergh and Amelia Earhart stopped at the site several times to talk to officials mapping out the field for Transcontinental Air Transport.

Most transcontinental flights stopped at Portair Field during the early years in order to refuel. A small village began at Portair and a transient relief camp made its home at the site. As the technology of plane construction improved the need for constant refueling decreased causing Portair Field to be bypassed while flights to Roswell, Albuquerque, Santa Fe, Denver and Oklahoma City increased.

Clovis also became important as a stopover on the Transcontinental

Air Transport (TAT). The route of the TAT was from Los Angeles to Clovis by plane, then from Clovis to Oklahoma by rail, next from Oklahoma to Ohio by plane, and then a final train trip to New York City arriving forty-eight hours earlier on the third day. The objective of the TAT was to half the time it took to cross the United States by using air travel.

During World War II the airport was used as a bomber base and home of the 16th Bombardment Operational Wing. The site also served as a training base for crews going to Europe. The Air Force was established in 1942 and in 1943 Portair Field was renamed Clovis Municipal Airport. The name changed again to Cannon Air Force Base and was named after General John Cannon who received his wings in 1922.

Clovis received minor fame in the 1950s as the site of the Norman Petty Recording Studio established by the pop musician. Buddy Holly and the Crickets and other singers from the era recorded at the studio. The Cricket's most famous song, *That'll Be the Day* was recorded at the Petty Studio.

The 2010 census lists Clovis' population at thirty seven thousand residents. The economy is made up of dairy, peanut and cotton farmers, cattle ranchers and the military base. The New Mexico Land Commissioner signed an agreement making Clovis the renewable energy center for wind and solar power on the eastern plains.

The town of Texico was platted by the AT&SF in 1902. Ira Taylor a section foreman for the Pecos Valley & Northeastern Railroad was the first settler on the site. By 1902 the town consisted of a post office, the Jenkins Hotel, a blacksmith shop, one store, and a restaurant and saloon. Texico was originally part of the XIT Ranch called Escavado meaning dugout in Spanish for the number of homesteaders surrounding the location.

The railroad considered several locations as the division point when laying out the towns on the eastern plains. A four-day battle occurred between Texico and Farwell, Texas as to which town would receive the distinction. Both towns were disappointed when the honor went to Clovis. Texico and Farwell are often referred to as the "Twin Cities."

Texico is the oldest town in Curry County and in 1902 buildings formed on either side of a dirt main street where rooms were twenty five cents a night and Harry's Café offered the best meals in town often consisting of fresh oysters, steaks and lamb chops. By 1925 Texico had a graduating class at the local high school of nine students.

By July of 1905 railroad crews were hard at work on the town of Texico and adjoining railroad tracks. The AT&SF bought all the lots four hundred feet wide across the town. Texico has been compared to Dodge City, Kansas in its earlier days as a tent city where crews prepared to lay track and the law had not yet arrived.

End of the track towns or beginning in the case of Texico (the AT&SF started laying track on both ends of the route and met in the middle) were notorious for their wild behavior although the railroad attempted to establish some control. Laws were passed prohibiting the establishment of a saloon within three miles of a new railroad town. Those ignoring the law were prosecuted.

Those owning early businesses in the town were from Amarillo, Hereford and the plains country of Texas. They were used to the isolated and wide open plains and saw opportunities for mercantile stores, for those wanting to start a newspaper or livery stable. Those wanting to hide from the law also came to the area establishing saloons, bordellos and gambling halls.

Information on the town in its early years is sketchy mainly because of disastrous fires in the community that ruined the newspaper files at both Texico and Farwell across the border in Texas. Many newspaper files were destroyed prior to 1912 in Clovis, but fortunately many early stories survived in the Portales newspapers.

The *Portales Herald* printed the following article about Texico in July of 1905, "Each week brings more contractors, men and railroad materials to Texico. Mr. Temple of Amarillo is the last contractor to arrive. His men are grading on the first mile out. Water is getting to be a scarce article at Texico and on the new railroad west. But the big machinery for the company is going down after more water. The railroad company had bought all the town lots on the strip over four hundred feet wide clear across the town, and is moving business houses and residences also, to make room for their extensive switch tracks south of town. They will soon have a post office at Blacktower sixteen miles west, on the line of the new road. The place will be called Newman and Mr. Bruce will be the postmaster. Norris and Wilson built a new house for the *Texico Trumpet* newspaper this week between the Racket Store and post office."

By 1905 Texico had become more civilized as a Mr. White had put in a new phone service, and the school system had a three-month school year in place. F.L. Loomis became the editor of the *Trumpet* newspaper and the community began to grow. Its location made the town a middle point when traveling between Clovis and Amarillo, Texas and points eastward.

In 1907 W.K. Simmons the former owner of a house of prostitution attacked J.C. Wells, a printer at the local newspaper. Mr. Wells entered the newspaper office and confronted Simmons about what was being printed in the newspaper and proceeded to knock him down with his fists.

Simmons intended to murder Wells, when he reached for his gun Wells grabbed a heavy stove poker and struck Simmons breaking his arm. But, Simmons tried to fire at Wells a second time, but Wells was standing six feet away and threw the poker at him again knocking the gun and his aim. The two struggled and Simmons fired the gun twice more, but Wells finally got the drop on him and ordered Simmons at gunpoint to follow him out of the building. By this time a crowd had gathered after hearing the shots and disturbance. Simmons escaped although he was eventually apprehended.

In 1912 the community was attracting new businesses. One was the Panhandle Trailer Company owned by Carl Penn. His company manufactured the Thunderbird camper. With new families moving into the farming community the railroad town had reached a population of five hundred and sixty nine by 1940.

Texico's population was one thousand in the 2008 census with ranching, farming and oil being the major economy. The community located between Clovis and Muleshoe, Texas is a pleasant place to stop and enjoy the scenery before heading east across the Texas plains.

10

Socorro, the Capitol Bar and Elfego Baca

Early Socorro. Author's collection.

Socorro, a Spanish word meaning help or aid was named by Onate and the first Spanish settlers traveling the Camino Real in 1598. The group nearly perished when they took the eighty mile shortcut known as the Jornada del Murerto (journey of the dead man). Upon reaching the Rio Grande River they were given food and water by the Piro Indians prompting Onate to supply the name.

The first catholic mission was established in 1626 and named Nuestra Senor de Socorro. A Spanish census lists six hundred people living in the vicinity. During the Pueblo Revolt the Spanish were pushed out of New Mexico for twelve years. Spanish refugees fleeing the revolt warned those living in Socorro as they rushed southward toward El Paso and reasonable safety. Socorro was destroyed during the Pueblo Revolt and many of the friendly Piro Indians killed.

The Spanish did not resettle Socorro for another one hundred and thirty seven years. In 1817 seventy residents from Belen petitioned for land in Socorro. They soon built the Mission of San Miguel de Socorro on the ruins of the Nuestra de Socorro. The settlement as others along the river developed into an agriculture and ranching area.

The San Miguel Church was finished in 1821 and the rest of the community grew around it. The original buildings were constructed in the style of the Spanish with thick walls and mud floors. Socorro, as all early communities along the Rio Grande River endured attacks by the Apache and Navajo Indians.

By the 1880s mining was active in the Magdalena Mountains, the San Mateos and Black Range where Hillsboro and Kingston were booming. The Billings Smelter was the principal smelter in New Mexico Territory and also processed more ore and silver in the central and southern portions of the territory. In the 1890s the Billings Smelter changed owners and became the Rio Grande Smelter Works a branch of a St. Louis company. The smelter eventually closed in 1896 causing a decline in Socorro's population and economy.

Before the turn of the twentieth century the Park, Grand Central and Windsor were three prominent hotels in town. The Grand Central was located east of the plaza and vacated in 1898. The Windsor Hotel resided on Manzanares Avenue and received most of the tourist trade of the time. After the hotel burned to the ground it was replaced with the Val Verde in 1919 and rebuilt near the same location.

The Park Hotel was one of the older hotels in town and boarded politicians and other distinguished visitors traveling the territory during this era. New Mexico Governor Lew Wallace the author of *Ben Hur* stayed at the hotel. In the 1960s the front lobby and main rooms making up the hotel were torn down and replaced by a Safeway-Ben Franklin building.

PARK HOTEL (FORMERLY CHAMBON HOTEL), SOCORRO, NEW MEXICO, G. M. BRASS, JR., OWNER.

CHAMBON HOTEL

NEW MEXICO'S HISTORICAL AND INTERESTING LANDMARK.

Park Hotel in Socorro. Author's collection.

For many years the Val Verde Hotel was the social center for Socorro County and much of New Mexico. The hotel held receptions, meetings, benefit bridge parties plus dances and college proms. It boasted a barber shop and beauty parlor and was a good location for fashion shows. The hotel contained sixty guest rooms, a dining room, large lobby and reading rooms.

Socorro began to boom in the 1880s when the population of the quiet ranching and farming community reached a thousand residents when gold and silver were officially discovered in the nearby mountains. When the AT&SF arrived, the population of the town exploded. During a six month period in 1881 there were three thousand mining claims filed at the Socorro County Courthouse.

The completion of railroad lines throughout the American frontier put stagecoaches out of business. Socorro was connected by stage to White Oaks to the east, a gold mining center reached by traveling through San Antonio, NM to the south in 1879. Established towns along the route vied for the trade at White Oaks and during the 1880s Socorro often competed with Las Vegas for this trade.

The stage ran regularly between Socorro and Magdalena. If riding all the way to the silver mining town of Kelly the trip cost $2.75 in 1883. The stage left Socorro on Mondays, Wednesdays and Fridays at 8:00 in the morning and returned to Socorro on alternate days at four in the afternoon.

Socorro had reached a population over three thousand before the turn of the twentieth century and during these years over thirty drinking places were established. The most famous of these is the Capitol Bar residing on the plaza in the center of the community. The Capitol was built in 1896 by two Italian brothers named Giovanni and Tobaschi Biavaschi. Giovanni had been a respected winemaker in Italy.

Later the brothers sold the bar to Amos Green who also served as the justice of the peace. He held court in the bar and jailed those found guilty in a back room. The jail is no longer part of the establishment but the bars are still visible through the windows. The bar was renamed the Green Front Bar after the judge. The establishment has gone by the names of the Biavaschi Saloon, the Club Bar, Gallegos Bar and Green Front Bar. Most saloon establishments went out of business during prohibition of course, but the Capitol was known as Green's Pool Hall during these years with gambling and a healthy bootlegging business on the side.

Fred Emilio moved to Socorro from Lincoln County in 1923 and had plans of going into the pool hall business with his friend Damien Padilla. Unfortunately, as soon as they had their pool hall up and running it was destroyed by a fire a few months after opening. Amos Green was looking for someone to assume management of the Green Front Bar and Emilio and Padilla took the position.

The bar soon became a favorite hangout for ranchers, miners and students attending the local School of Mines. Fred Emilio kept a secret stash of the finest Kentucky whiskeys to share with special friends and customers frequenting the bar. The bar became even more popular when the building was updated with modern restrooms, a dance floor and knotty-pine paneling on the walls and ceiling.

During the prohibition years there was a trap door behind the bar leading to the basement and an escape route from the police. At the end of prohibition the bar became the first legalized bar in Socorro. The name was changed to the Capitol Bar in 1937. The Capitol Bar is the oldest bar in Socorro, and the only one to survive the turbulent years of Socorro's early history when there was a bar on every corner.

The New Mexico Institute of Mining & Technology is located in Socorro and was first established as the New Mexico School of Mines in 1889. The college offers over thirty bachelor degrees specializing in mining and petroleum programs. Students from all over the United States attend school and receive a first-rate education. The surrounding area provides recreational opportunities in the nearby Cibola National Forest.

The 2010 census lists Socorro's population as seventeen thousand residents. The community has long been the county seat of Socorro County, the second largest county in New Mexico and at one time included both Socorro and Catron County, the state's largest county. The community remains a supply center and college town.

One of Socorro's most infamous residents was Elfego Baca. Law and order were often lacking on the American frontier. Rustlers, outlaw gangs, unruly cowboys and renegade Apache and Navajo Indians made trouble for early settlers on New Mexico's frontier.

Frontier lawmen frequently served as the only law for hundreds of miles and at times their control tactics were considered controversial. A few famous lawmen were Wyatt Earp, Seth Bullock, El Paso's Dallas Stoudenmire and Elgego Baca from Socorro County. Baca and Pat Garrett are the two most well-known sheriffs involved in law and order along Highway 60.

According to a local story Elfego Baca was born on a baseball field in Socorro. His mother enjoyed playing ball and interrupted a game in 1865 to give birth to Elfego. His father Francisco moved their family to Topeka, Kansas when Elfego was an infant. Over a decade later after the death of his mother, Elfego and Francisco returned to New Mexico Territory where Francisco accepted a job as city marshal of Belen.

While serving as city marshal, Francisco shot and killed two cowboys refusing to stop disturbing the town by running their horses up and down the streets and shooting at store windows. A local court felt he went too far, and he was incarcerated in the Los Lunas Jail. Elfego reportedly dug a hole in the roof and freed his father who then escaped into hiding.

Baca returned to Socorro and established a reputation as a competent gunman. In 1884 when he was nineteen years old he bought a mail order badge and proclaimed himself a lawman. His first job was in Frisco, now Reserve where a group of cowboys from the Slaughter Ranch were hurrahing and terrorizing the town.

Fricso, as most frontier towns was a wild town in the 1880s and claimed over a dozen bars and bordellos. The town favored cattlemen arriving daily. It did not take Baca long to discover a cowboy named McCarty was the ring leader of a group of cowboys habitually racing up and down Main Street and shooting at anything they noticed. He approached McCarty, stuck a gun to his head and ordered him to walk toward the jail. He hoped to return to Socorro with his prisoner the following morning.

John Slaughter, the ranch owner and foreman where McCarty was employed confronted Baca near the jail and ordered the release of the prisoner. Baca refused and warned the cowboys he would count to three and start shooting. They called his bluff, and his first shots caused Slaughter's horse to flip over crushing him in the process. Baca was able to lock his prisoner in the Frisco Jail.

A justice of the peace in Frisco agreed to try McCarty. He was fined five dollars for disturbing the peace and set free. According to most sources at least eighty cowboys awaited Baca outside the courtroom. A second battle erupted and for the next thirty-six hours Baca did not back down until late afternoon of the second day of the fight. A deputy sheriff named Ross convinced Baca to turn himself in and return to Socorro with him. Baca agreed to surrender if he could keep his gun for the return trip.

Baca spent the next four months in the Socorro County Jail. He was eventually acquitted on two counts of murder. Jail time changed Baca, and he decided to become a genuine law enforcement officer and criminal lawyer. The New Mexico Bar Association allowed him to start practicing law in 1894. He served as assistant district attorney, district attorney and school superintendent plus county clerk and mayor of Socorro. He is most often remembered for his contributions while serving as sheriff of Socorro County.

11

Magdalena, Butch Cassidy, Kelly and Alamo

The history of Magdalena is made up of stories about Spanish explorers, Apache and Navajo Indians, miners, speculators, ranchers and cattle drives. The discovery of silver ore at Kelly in 1863 and the railroad led to the development of Magdalena. Settlement began in 1875 but it would take another nine years for the town to be officially established.

The following year the AT&SF built a spur line to Magdalena causing the community to boom as a major shipping point for ore and later livestock on the Magdalena Driveway. The town known as Magdalena Mines had a post office by 1878 and a total of forty seven residents. They were all male and listed their occupations as nine laborers, thirty-six miners, one doctor and one blacksmith.

The town took its name from the distinct peak south of town named by a priest and group of Spanish soldiers in the 1540s looking for safety while being pursued by the Apache. There are two versions to the meaning of the peak. One, the mountain reminded the group of a mountain back in Spain and they named the peak "La Sierra de Magdalena" in its honor. In the other version the group saw the face of Mary Magdalene appear on the side of the mountain and named the peak after her.

A legend began that no harm would come to those in the shadow of Magdalena Peak. Agnes Morley Cleveland described the peak in 1886 in her book *No Life for a Lady*. "There is a legend that Lady Magdalena Mountain was a sanctuary respected by Indians, where fugitives, whether deservedly or not, found refuge from pursing enemies," Cleveland wrote. "The legend did not hold as many a pursued man fell before his nemesis in the streets of Magdalena."

F.G. Bartlett built the first business in Magdalena in 1883 and began buying and selling wool. His Ranch Supply Company of Magdalena was one of the oldest businesses in the area. Bartlett helped organize the First National Bank and he owned the Liberty Hotel.

By May of 1885 the foundation for the train depot and the stock pens were started. Magdalena would become known as "Trails End" and a well-known livestock shipping point. Many businesses were in operation in Magdalena by 1886 including four saloons, a schoolhouse and church, two lumber yards, two blacksmith shops, three restaurants, two livery stables, a drug and hardware store plus a sash and door establishment.

Cleveland described Magdalena in 1886 when her family spent the night in the original Magdalena Hotel. She wrote, "We arrived in Magdalena February 1886...please give us a room that is not directly over the barroom my mother stipulated to the hotel-keeper when we arrived. I'm afraid those bullets will come up through the floor. It was years afterwards before Magdalena gathered itself together and made it a misdemeanor to shoot within the town limits."

Much of the original town site of Magdalena was destroyed by fire. More than half the town burned in 1900 when a lack of water prevented firefighters from halting the blaze. Until 1920 the fire department consisted of a few volunteers with a horse-drawn cart and water tank. The fires often overran the resources.

After a series of fires in 1918 that ended in the original Magdalena Hotel burning to the ground, the fire department decided to buy an actual fire engine. The new engine arrived in 1922 when the California Hotel was destroyed by fire. The recently acquired fire engine had little effect on the fire without the water needed to operate the pump.

Magdalena's population declined during these years, and many vacant buildings were burned in a group of suspicious fires nicknamed the insurance fires. The Wilson Hotel and Catholic Church burned in the 1930s, but by the forties most of the houses in Magdalena were constructed of adobe and brick and not as easy to catch fire.

Drought and another water shortage caused fire problems in 1952 when the historic Becker-Mactavish Store burned to the ground and another portion of the original block of town. Susan Lee describes how the town's people felt about the loss of the historic store.

She writes in her book *These Also Served*, "When I moved to Magdalena the store was known as the Becker-Mactavish Company. Mactavish came to Magdalena when Magdalena was a thriving cattle and mining town. The Kelly Mines were in full operation. The stockmen for over a hundred miles came to Magdalena to ship their cattle and buy supplies. The old store was recently burned and when you get to Magdalena nowadays the first thing you miss is the Mactavish Store."

Becker-Mactavish Store. Author's Collection.

John Sinclair Mactavish immigrated to Magdalena from Scotland in 1897. He found employment at the Becker-Blackwell Company co-founded by Gustav Becker the brother of pioneer, Belen mercantile owner John Becker. Mactavish later bought out Blackwell and became co-owner of the establishment with Becker and the name of the business was changed to Becker-Mactavish Company.

In 1917 the Becker-Mactavish Store advertised wool, hides, pelts, farm implements, Studebaker automobiles and Goodyear Tires. Mactavish and Becker did in Magdalena what John Becker accomplished in Belen and became the guiding force behind the establishment and growth of the town.

Gustav Becker, the other co-owner of the store moved to Springerville, Arizona where he went into partnership with his brother Julius and established the Becker Brothers Store an important supply center for ranchers, farmers and military posts between Socorro and Arizona. The store would later be called the Gustav Becker Store and then merely Becker Mercantile Store. Gustav's store was also destroyed by fire in 1964.

The Becker brothers and other merchants who had the money and ability to establish mercantile stores on the American frontier often became the politicians and most wealthy business men in town. They had to possess sturdy wagons and teams of oxen and mules to pull the heavy wagons across the country. They transported their supplies from mercantile store to mercantile store to outfit those living in the more isolated areas. These early businesses contained everything needed on the frontier and were often the only supply centers for hundreds of miles.

The new fire engine came close to burning in the Mactavish fire, but luckily someone noticed the tires were smoldering, the fire hoses were melting before the water could reach the fire and the gas tank was unusually hot. The engine was moved in time and water was transported from Socorro by railroad tank cars when the fire spread to the Aragon Hotel nearby.

The Hammond Hotel caught fire in 1965 but was controlled before spreading. A few years later, the Aragon Theater and Pythian Hotel burned. Even as late as 1983 another fire swept through the remaining portion of the old, business district. The McDonald building was lost, but firefighters saved the Salome Store in the same block.

Susan Lee writes about moving to Magdalena, "In 1913 we moved to Magdalena. Both Magdalena and Kelly were thriving towns. Kelly was noted for its mines and Magdalena was the largest shipping point in this part of the West. Living in Magdalena afforded me the opportunity of meeting and knowing many of the old timers. There was Bob Lewis, sheriff; Johnnie McDonald, stockman and Mr. Wildenstein, the blacksmith."

Lee goes on to describe Wildenstein's Blacksmith Shop and its importance to early Magdalena. "I remember Mr. Wildenstein's Blacksmith Shop in 1913. There were very few cars in those days and no garages at all. I used to pass the shop most every day and loved to watch the horses being shod or see the sparks fly from pieces of metal Mr. Wildenstein would be hammering on the anvil. It was about the busiest place in town."

Magdalena was incorporated in 1918 and the village elected Jose Aragon as their first mayor. Aragon, another early settler instrumental to the development of early Magdalena was the proprietor of the Aragon Hotel. Aragon and Mactavish worked together to acquire bells for the Community and Catholic Churches and traveled to a factory on the East coast where they were purchased. Mactavish chose a bell in G major for the Community Church and Aragon a bell in G minor for the Catholic Church and the bells once installed rank in harmony.

Billy the Kid and the Ketchum brothers are most often associated with the outlaw history of New Mexico Territory; yet Butch Cassidy, the Sundance Kid and members of the Wild Bunch Gang contributed to the history of southern New Mexico and the once booming towns of Alma, Mogollon and Magdalena in the late 1890s. The outlaws used the WS Ranch near Alma as their headquarters where they worked as cowboys when hiding from the Pinkerton Detectives.

Cattle rustling, a major problem on the American frontier sparked controversy from Wyoming to New Mexico. Powerful ranchers belonging to the Cheyenne Social Club in Wyoming hired gunmen from other states to terrorize homesteaders in the Johnson County War. John Chisum, used armed cowboys to protect his cattle herds along the Pecos River in southern New Mexico; and Captain William French hired Butch Cassidy and members of the Wild Bunch to work on the WS Ranch in 1898 where the outlaws quickly gained control of French's rustling problems.

Captain French, a foreman and part-owner of the WS Ranch suspected his own cowhands of stealing WS cattle and fired the crew. A few days later, a man giving his name as Jim Lowe stopped at the ranch looking for work and

French immediately hired him. He soon placed Lowe in a foreman position not realizing his real named was Leroy Parker more commonly known as Butch Cassidy. The Sundance Kid or Harry Longabaugh used the name Tom Capehart while employed on the ranch. The outlaws had little trouble gaining control of those rustling French's cows, and some sources pointed out his cattle herd actually increased while Butch Cassidy was the foreman of the WS Ranch.

The WS Ranch was well suited for the needs of the outlaw gang. The Mexican border a few days ride to the south and railheads at Magdalena and Silver City provided easy escape routes in case the Pinkerton detectives discovered their location. The gang had hideouts and caches of horses and supplies at various sites along the Outlaw Trail from New Mexico to Montana. They would split up after a heist and meet months to a year later after dividing the money.

William French described the behavior of the Wild Bunch on a cattle drive to the Magdalena railhead in the book *Recollections of a Western Ranchman*. He wrote, "When they got to the road they were most decorous. There was no such thing as drinking or gambling or shooting up the town. Strict discipline was always maintained, and I was frequently congratulated by the merchants of Magdalena on having such a well-behaved outfit."

French and others the group worked for commented on their work ethic and abilities with horses and cattle. French wrote the following about Butch Cassidy's trailing of WS cattle to Magdalena, "The way he handled those cattle over that long and dusty trail of nearly two hundred miles was a revelation. Frequently, they had to go as much as seventy-five miles without water, but he never dropped a hoof, and there was no tail to his herd when they arrived at the road."

Butch worked as a foreman for Captain William French and hired Elzy Lay, and other pals as hands. In July of 1899 Lay, Sam Ketchum and Will Carver robbed a Colorado & Southern train at Folsom near the Colorado border. The robbery, poorly executed, landed Elzy Lay in the New Mexico Territorial Prison. Sam Ktechum was killed and Carver escaped. In October, Carver used money taken in the robbery in an Alma saloon alerting the Pinkerton detectives to the gang's location.

Captain French was informed by detectives that Butch Cassidy and

Jim Lowe were the same person and cowboys in his employment had robbed a train near Folsom. French did not turn in the outlaws, but they left the ranch soon afterwards.

No stories or exploits are linked to the outlaw gang in southern New Mexico after the turn of the twentieth century, and they probably never returned to the WS Ranch. They moved their operations to Wyoming, Nevada and Texas before moving to Argentina and making an effort to become respectable ranchers. Butch, Sundance and Etta Place the wife or girlfriend of Sundance created a prosperous ranch hoping to avoid their outlaw pasts.

The Wild Bunch spent a relatively short time at the WS Ranch compared to their other hideout locations. Only ruins and a cemetery remain at the town site of Alma in New Mexico's Mogollon Mountains where Jim Lowe and Tom Capehart made a name for themselves as loyal and dependable ranch-hands. Butch and the Wild Bunch were one of the last outlaw gangs to survive into the twentieth century.

The Magdalena Driveway was an important means of getting cattle and sheep to market. The one hundred and twenty mile driveway was set aside when ranchers in the area petitioned for it to remain an official driveway and therefore not available for homesteading. The driveway was used to trail livestock from eastern Arizona and southern New Mexico to the railhead in Magdalena.

In 1970 David Farr was the last rancher to trail cattle to the railhead by using the driveway. In an interview with BLM archaeologist Brenda Wilkinson he explains a little history of the Magdalena Driveway.

According to the interview Farr always took three horses on cattle drives. He explains his reasons, "You'd ride one in the morning, and one in the afternoon and one at night, and have an extra horse," he explained.

Those trailing livestock to the railhead started the drives on the same date each year. "For years we started the drives on October 20 but in later years the date was changed to October 18," explained Farr. The herds would line up on the trail and the Santa Fe Railroad agent in Magdalena ran the operations once the herds arrived in town.

"It was a nightmare when we got the cattle to Magdalena. Those steam engines would let off steam and the sound would turn the cows. With dogs barking and cowboys yelling it was a real job to get those cows up to the corral," stated Farr.

According to Farr the driveway fell into disuse during the years prior to World War II as people were starting to use trucks to transport their cattle to market. "During the war people returned to using the stock highway again due to shortages in fuel, steel and rubber," pointed out Farr.

There was a system once the cattle were corralled. "The cattle stood in the corral overnight for twelve hours or so and they were weighed in the morning. Next, you had to wait for the train to arrive and then loaded the herds on the cars," stated Farr.

The cowboys spent their hard earned money on alcohol and vices provided in the cattle town. Most of the time they remained in town for days until their money was gone. According to Farr, "Many times all the cowboys got drunk and many times my brothers and I took all the horses home."

The Magdalena Old Timer's Reunion began in 1971. Cecil Owsley a retired rodeo rider invited a few old friends to a calf ropin, pot-luck and barbecue. Over a hundred people attended his first get together and it soon developed into an annual event. Owsley grew up on the Pueblo Springs Ranch north of Magdalena. He left in 1924 when the bottom dropped out of the cattle market and worked as a rodeo performer. He became friends with Slim Pickens, Gene Autry and other well-known circuit riders from the era and was inducted into the Cowboy Hall of Fame.

The Old Timers' Reunion has activities for the old and young with parades, barbecues, rodeo events, a crafts fair, school reunions, street dances and booths. People come for hundreds of miles to join in the fun, as they did when the community was the largest livestock shipping point in the region.

As of the 2012 Census Magdalena has a population of nine hundred and twenty six residents and artists have restored what is left of the old business district. The stockyards remain on the north end of town where thousands of head of livestock were trailed on the Magdalena Driveway as evidence of the town's frontier roots. With a little imagination, a faint image of Mary Magdalene still appears in the afternoon light near Magdalena Peak.

Kelly, a ghost town southeast of Magdalena was once an active, silver mining community with three thousand residents, two schools, three churches and dance halls open all night and a moving picture parlor. At one time, Kelly was the most prosperous silver, mining town in New Mexico.

Mountain Queen Saloon in Kelly, New Mexico. Author's collection.

Silver Ore was discovered near Kelly in 1863 by a Union solder named Pete Kingsinger. It was not uncommon for soldiers stationed at forts in the area to prospect on the side and many settled in the area when their tour of duty ended. At the end of the Civil War, Kingsinger decided to try his luck in the northeast corner of the territory in the silver mines near Elizabethtown. While there he told Colonel J.S. Hutchason about his findings in the Magdalena Mountains.

Hutchason is credited with discovering what would become the Kelly, Graphic and Juanita Mines and starting the silver boom in the Magdalena Mountains. By 1886, Huchason or "Old Hutch" had the mines in operation and took a partner named Andy Kelly. Kelly only worked the mine for a short time but the area has retained the name.

Miners hearing of the new silver strike arrived in droves and by the 1870s had laid out the town site and named it Kelly after the successful mine. There was little room for the growing population and hotel owners helped to deal with the housing shortage by renting beds in eight hours shifts.

James McGee, one of Kelly's early citizens owned and operated the assay office, a saloon, store and café. He was instrumental in the development of Kelly during the boom years between 1880 and 1920. He first moved to the area from Wisconsin and worked at the Rosedale Mine in the foothills of the San Mateo Mountains southwest of Magdalena.

Victorio, Nana, Geronimo and various Apache tribes often hunted and camped in the San Mateo Mountains and conflict with miners was not uncommon. While working on the Rosedale claim alone one afternoon, McGee was attacked by a small group of Apache Indians and an arrow embedded in his back where he could not remove it. He was able to ride horse back to Magdalena and have the arrow removed. While recuperating at the home of a friend he decided to move to Kelly where he remained and prospered.

In 1876, Hutchason sold the Kelly Mines to Gustav Billings for forty five thousand dollars. Billings had connections, money and influence and is responsible for the early development of both Kelly and Magdalena. He made a fortune in the smelting business in Colorado before building another smelter in Socorro in 1833. Billings persuaded the AT&SF to build a two-mile spur to Kelly in 1884. The twenty six mile Magdalena Branch was closed in the 1970s but in its early history it was referred to as the best paying railroad route the AT&SF had.

Kelly boomed for fifteen years before the silver crash of the 1890s and the closing of silver mines throughout the American frontier. Billings had to close the Socorro Smelter in 1893 and Kelly's silver boom started to fade. A few years later, zinc carbonate or smithsonite, a pigment found in paints was discovered.

Sherwood-Williams Paint Company bought the Graphic Mine in 1904 and the mine produced until 1928 and was worth more than twenty one million dollars. Kelly was the leading zinc producer in the state. Ruins, a church, cemetery, and an abandoned mine are all that remain of Kelly. Even the buildings making up the original town site have vanished. The Kelly Church is the only structure left standing in the once booming mining town.

Highway 169 intersects with Highway 60 on the west end of Magdalena and heads north along the Gallinas Mountains in the direction of the Alamo Navajo Indian Reservation. The Alamo Reservation is almost as isolated as it was when established in 1866 with few roads and modern conveniences.

The Alamo Navajo Reservation is made up of members of both the Navajo and Mescalero Apache tribes. Scouts working for Kit Carson during the Indian removal campaign to Bosque Redondo in the 1860s and their families were placed on a smaller reservation away from those sent to Bosque Redondo at Fort Sumner. Over the past century the two tribes have integrated and are now known as the Alamo Navajo tribe.

The land making up the Alamo Reservation includes an area close to one hundred miles and in the last census had two thousand residents. The reservation is adjacent to the Acoma Indian Reservation to the north, the Cibola National Forest to the west and east plus ranch land and open space between the reservation and Magdalena. The land making up the reservation is four-tenths of one percent of the total area of the Navajo Nation.

The Navajo tribe is the largest in the United States and has the biggest reservation in the country. The Navajo and Apache probably arrived in the Southwest between 1200 and 1300. They were a nomadic tribe living by raiding and hunting. Although the Navajo took Mexican children and women as captives, the group as a whole co-existed peacefully with the first Americans to settle on their homeland.

With the establishment of Fort Defiance and Fort Wingate in the 1850s near present-day Gallup, the relationship between the Navajo and Americans began to deteriorate. In September of 1861 conditions became even worse when thirty Navajo were massacred on orders of Colonel Manuel Chaves the commander of Fort Wingate because the soldiers and Navajo disagreed over the outcome of a horse race.

General James Carleton New Mexico's army commander wrote a plan to remove Navajo and Mescalero Apache tribes to a reservation on the Pecos River and Fort Sumner was soon erected. The reservation selected for the two tribes was forty square miles. Many tried stopping the creation of the reservation because of its poor water source and lack of firewood. But Carleton was determined to try his experiment and the government went ahead with the newly organized reservation.

Four hundred Mescalero Apache were first moved to the site, and then nearly nine thousand Navajo were forced to walk over three hundred miles to Bosque Redondo. This tragic time in their history is known as the Long Walk. Many died en route and hundreds more died while they were incarcerated on the reservation. They were not allowed to leave the reservation for hunting purposes, and when their crops failed many of them starved to death.

By 1865 everyone agreed the reservation system had been a mistake and the Mescalero slipped away back to the area surrounding Sierra Blanca in the Sacramento Mountains. The Navajo would endure the reservation for another three years until 1868 when they were allowed to return to their homeland, although the area they had first inhabited was drastically reduced in size.

The Navajo and Mescalero Apache were luckier than most of the tribes that would follow them onto reservations. They were both allowed to return to their homeland. The U.S. Government issued rations and sheep to the Navajo. They were able to prosper through their flocks of sheep and produced wool, wonderful rugs and jewelry.

Alamo is part of the Navajo Nation and is governed much like counties within the state of New Mexico. Elected officials from Alamo make government decisions affecting the tribe. Alamo is not quite as isolated as it was at one time and now has a health clinic, emergency medical services, a senior citizen's center and courthouse.

The town recently acquired a mini-mart and the community's first gas station. The Alamo Reservation is made up of sixty three thousand acres of land and over two thousand residents. Yet, due to the isolation of the small community the people have retained many of their customs and the use of the Navajo language.

12

Datil, the Navajo Lodge, the Apache and Montague Stevens

Navajo Lodge. Author's Collection.

Datil is located thirty-eight miles west of Magdalena and began its history as a mercantile store and stage stop established by Levi and Fred Baldwin in 1884. It became an important crossroads along the Magdalena Driveway until the 1950s.

The Baldwin brothers built the original town site of Datil located a mile from the town's present location. Levi Baldwin became the first postmaster in 1886. Agnes Morley Cleveland, author of *No Life for a Lady*, described Datil in 1886 when her family first moved to the area.

"That night we stopped at Baldwin's stage station. It was an adobe house with a two-story log structure at one end. Half a dozen doors opened from the façade. The log end of the building was a store and the other end a hotel."

Members of the Sixth Cavalry built and staffed Camp Datil between 1884 and 1886. The fort was abandoned when Geronimo surrendered in 1886 and the last Apache raids were brought under control. Currently Datil resides at the site of the old fort. Cleveland describes an incident when a courier came to the ranch and warned the family that Geronimo was this side of Quemado. The group made it to Baldwin's Ranch ten miles away but the Apache went south instead.

Datil Well, west of Datil was once a watering hole along the Beefsteak or Hoof Highway from eastern Arizona to the stockyards at Magdalena. During its heyday, the Magdalena Driveway was as important as the Goodnight-Loving and other cattle trails crisscrossing the country. The driveway forked at Datil. One route went south in the direction of Horse Springs and Reserve, and the other continued to the Arizona border.

The Morley family arrived in the area soon after the initial settlement of the town. In a meadow a few miles west of Datil on what was once the Morley Ranch are the gravesite and monument to the Morley family. The Morleys would settle near Datil in 1885. Morley was an engineer with the AT&SF Railroad and was instrumental in the railroad winning the right of way through Raton Pass. He also managed the extensive Maxwell Land Grant in the northern portion of the state and was the editor of the *Cimarron News*.

Morley was originally buried in Las Vegas, New Mexico on January 8, 1883. His funeral was held at the Plaza Hotel and well attended by friends, politicians and dignitaries. His friends had a monument erected to his memory and placed at the gravesite. Over a hundred years later in 1993, after the monument was continually vandalized, his grandson Norman Cleveland moved his remains and the monument to the family ranch.

Ray Morley met Ada McPherson at the state university in Iowa City, Iowa after he had served with General Sherman during the Civil War. Morley was orphaned at an early age and raised on his uncle's Iowa farm. Ada, on the other hand was accustomed to a life of wealth and ease, as her father Marcus McPherson was a distinguished lawyer and politician. Ray and Ada had three children named Lorraine, Agnes and Ray.

Morley was accidentally killed in a shooting accident while working for the Mexican Central Railroad between Nogales and Guymas, Mexico in 1883. Ada later married a man named Floyd Jarrett who encouraged her to sink her remaining resources into purchasing a ranch near Datil and then over-stocked it with expensive, registered cattle. By 1889, Jarrett had deserted the family and they had no choice but to stay and make their ranching enterprise work.

The Morley family had the pioneer spirit needed to survive on land still occupied by the Apache when they first set up their isolated ranch house. The Morley children thrived on the land, and the family stuck it out and in later years even prospered. Ada, having little experience running a cattle ranch often relied on her children and neighbors to help her with cattle roundups and trailing her herd to the railhead in Magdalena.

The family built an impressive log cabin often referred to as the White house of Datil Canyon where hospitality was always found by friends and those needing a place to stay. The family started to build the log cabin shortly after settling in Datil Canyon. They used ox teams to drag tall, ponderosa pine trees to the canyon bottom where experienced axe men were waiting to hew and fit the logs. A two-story, ten-room log cabin was soon erected, carpeting installed and the inside whitewashed and hung with paintings and family portraits.

In the 1920s when the house fell into disuse, Ray Morley had it taken apart and moved piece by piece to Datil where it was reassembled and renamed the Navajo Lodge and catered to tourists on the ocean-to-ocean highway. He also hired Navajo families to live and work at the site. Tourists were able to watch Navajo women weave blankets they could later purchase. Tourist courts and camping spots near Highway 60 were common for those traveling the transcontinental highway for the first time.

Susan Lee writes about the Navajo Lodge in her book *These Also Served,* "It was beautiful. The office had a huge fireplace and the Navajo culture was carried out by huge Navajo rugs hanging from the railings and balcony. The great Lazy Susan type dining room added zest to the meals, as it was so unusual in those times and people loved it." The Navajo Lodge was destroyed by fire in 1944 taking a part of the Morley family with it.

A woman named Frances Minerva Nunnery would later clean away the burned debris at the site and rebuild. She wanted to "run one of those roadside joints," as she pointed out in the book *Woman of the Century* by Dawkins. She wrote, "The lobby of my lodge, with the bar at one end, was about twenty-five to thirty feet. It had a huge fireplace and everybody's brand from the ranches around embedded in the stones. Later I added eight slab cabins." The roadside business continues to cater to those traveling Highway 60 although the name has changed to the Eagle Guest Ranch.

The Morley children all left their mark on the world. Lorraine Reynolds opened the first schoolhouse in Datil in 1917 and later had to homestead the land where the schoolhouse was located in order to keep it open. Her log cabin and schoolhouse were the start of the town of Datil. Her sister Agnes Morley Cleveland wrote magazine and newspaper articles and published two books, *Satan's Revenge* and her most well-known book *No Life for a Lady.* Over seventy-five years after its publication the book continues to sell as a popular account of the early settlement of the Magdalena and Datil areas.

Ray Morley was sent to the East coast to school and ended up with a degree in civil engineering. He also played and coached football for the Columbia University School of Mines. Later, he returned to the family ranch near Datil where he ran one of the largest and most extensive cattle and sheep operations in the state. Some sources say he leased another six hundred and forty acres from the U.S. Forest Service. He was also one of the founders of the New Mexico Stock Growers Association. Upon his death his ashes were spread over the land he had loved so well.

Another interesting character making up the history of the area was Montague Stevens, a one-armed Englishman and rancher near Datil who was one of the first and last to actively hunt grizzly bears. He embraced life on the American frontier and befriended western artist Frederick Remington, chased Apache with Indian fighter General George Crook and corresponded with Teddy Roosevelt.

Stevens an avid hunter first visited the United States from England in 1880 while on a hunting vacation in Wyoming. After graduating from Cambridge College with a degree in law, he returned the following year on a second vacation and decided to remain in the United States.

He moved to New Mexico Territory and went into the ranching business. He established ranches near Alma, Reserve and Datil with his ranch headquarters at Horse Springs. The land was still ruled by the Apache, renegade Mexicans and the grizzly bear, so those early settlers had to be tough and determined.

Stevens published a book in 1942 titled *Meet Mr. Grizzly* and wrote about his move to New Mexico Territory, "It was in the fall of 1882 that I bought my first ranches from early settlers, and so little was known of New Mexico in the East that I was several times asked if we have monkeys and parrots here. I have ranches scattered over an area of some eighty miles, generally known as the SU Ranches, the SU being my cattle brand." He also raised sheep as verified by the name of his ranch a few years later, SU Ranches & Shropshire Sheep Company.

Grizzly bears were a major problem for Stevens and early settlers near Datil. They often attacked without warning and took livestock and supplies. Stevens and his ranch foreman Dan Gatlin started training hounds to hunt grizzlies in 1889. They had a hard time in the beginning as the hounds would only track baited traps and were afraid of grizzlies.

By trial and error, Stevens and Gatlin raised an exceptional group of hunting dogs. They consistently tracked down grizzly bears when other hounds failed. Stevens described his pack of dogs in his book, "I had a number of different breeds of dogs. Besides the wolf hounds, I had a Great Dane, an English bob-tailed sheep dog, an English mastiff, a greyhound, two Scotch deer hounds, Scotch collies, and a various assortment of terriers, including Scotch, Irish, fox and bull terriers."

Steven's neighbors were skeptical of the abilities of his hunting pack in the beginning as related in his book, "While it was generally admitted that

I had a well-trained pack of hounds, doubts were frankly expressed that it would be possible for hounds to catch a bear, without any previous experience in hunting them."

Most hunters used only one or two dogs, but Stevens usually had between eight and ten. There were several reasons for Stevens using so many dogs. He felt they were encouraged to do their best when in a group. He explained his reasoning, "They might get crippled or tender-footed, so that if I depended on only two hounds, I might suddenly find myself without any hounds at all."

Stevens started his grizzly hunting pack with five bloodhounds named Sleuth, Psyche, Rufus, Rudolph and Inveed. He had two wolf hounds he referred to as the "slow trail dogs" named Panther and Wolf and a Great Dane. He writes about the dogs, "There was Princess, the Great Dane, whom I regarded as a sort of mother ship to the pack and any dog misbehaving was put under her care by being necked to her as punishment."

He had a fox terrier named Twist and three bull terriers nicknamed Grip, Nap and Biz. He explains his reasons for taking the bull terriers on a hunt. "There were also the three bull terriers, which I took along, not that they were of any particular use, but because I didn't have the heart to leave them behind, as I knew how they loved to scrap." Later he added a greyhound to the pack the only one of his dogs who could keep up with and turn a grizzly.

The first time Stevens took his hounds hunting grizzly, he shot the bear as soon as the pack had it treed and allowed it to fall among them. He was hoping they would start to pick up the grizzly scent on their own. He wrote, "I was particularly careful to kill the bear, as the hounds had never fought one before, and if he were only wounded and full of fight, some of them might have gotten hurt, in which case they would probably become bear-shy." On this same hunting trip, Stevens and his pack of dogs treed and killed five more grizzly bears.

Bounties were offered on troublesome grizzlies, and Stevens describes two grizzlies and the naming of Bear Trap Canyon in the San Mateo Mountains. He writes, "On a mountain thirty miles southwest of Magdalena, two grizzlies had been killing a good number of cattle, and a generous bounty was offered to anyone who could kill them. Two trappers, therefore, decided to try to catch a big grizzly in a bear trap, so they camped near the place where the tracks of these grizzlies seemed to show up the most and set their trap."

They waited outside the trap for over a week but did not see the grizzlies. Next, they built a small log cabin, about eight feet by ten feet with sturdy, log walls. A trap door was placed at one end and a deer carcass at the other. When the trappers returned the next morning, the trap had been sprung and was empty. They discovered another grizzly had dug under the trap from the outside and helped to free the one trapped inside. They both escaped and since the area has been referred to as Bear Trap Canyon.

Stevens quit hunting grizzlies when his favorite hunting dogs accidentally ate poisoned baits and he comforted them while they died. His ideas about hunting the silvertips changed as reflected in his writing. "As soon as I became resigned to the loss of my hounds and derived some consolation from the fact that there were few grizzlies left to hunt in the section of the Rocky Mountains over which I had hunted, and feeling that I had already had my full share of them, from that time on, I became a zealous convert to their preservation, to prevent so noble an animal from extinction."

Stevens did not prevent the extinction of the grizzly bear in New Mexico but actually contributed to their demise. He enjoyed the hunt too much and the experiences he shared with his pack of hunting dogs to give up stalking the grizzly until he had to do so. As most hunters who spend time observing the grizzly he had a deep respect for the bear.

Since the grizzly was a problem for those settling the American frontier, the majestic animal was shot, trapped, poisoned and hunted to extinction. Grizzlies only remain in the states of Alaska, Washington, Idaho, Montana and Wyoming. The last grizzly bear in New Mexico was killed in 1931 in the Mogollon Mountains near Silver City.

Datil is currently made up of the Eagle Guest Ranch and gas station located on the south side of Highway 60 where the Navajo Lodge once stood. It is the main gathering place for ranchers and others living in the isolated country. Datil named for the yucca seedpods that resembled dates to the Spanish was named Datil the Spanish word for date. In the 2010 census Datil had fifty-four residents.

13

Pie Town, the Lost Adams Diggings and One-Room Schoolhouses

Pie Town in 1940. Author's collection.

Pie Town, located on Highway 60 eighty-four miles west of Socorro, exists today because of pie and the Homestead Act. Originally named Norman's Place, the town began its history in 1922 as the mining claim of Clyde Norman. When the mining venture became unprofitable, he built a gas station where he would later sell homemade pies on the side.

Norman sold gas, oil, groceries and at first doughnuts made at a bakery in Datil. When there was an increase in automobile traffic and cowboys coming in from local ranches, the demand was more than the bakery could handle. Next, according to one story Norman took pie baking lessons from a neighbor, and after a little practice became well-known for his pies and changed the name of the business to Pie Town.

Two years later, Norman formed a partnership with Harmon Craig who would later buy him out and expand the pie making end of the business. Craig married Theodora Baugh, who had homesteaded land near Quemado with a former husband before he deserted her and their two daughters in Magdalena.

Theodora taught school in Mogollon and later worked as a cook on a ranch near Pie Town where she met Craig and they were married in Socorro in 1924. She would bake cookies, cakes and pies for her husband's roadside business and Pie Town became a popular stop and resting place along Highway 60.

Craig provided one hundred and sixty acres for a town site and encouraged homesteaders to move to the area. He even traveled to Mountainair and observed their process for the production of pinto beans before building the Bean House and installing bean cleaning equipment to help the homesteaders.

In Pie Town's early years the stage made a round trip daily through town and stopped at Craig's store and post office. The stage was outfitted with extra room for carrying packages, mail, newspapers, people and even crates of chickens. Since there were no phones or electricity at this time in Pie Town, the stage was the main form of communication in the area.

Pie Town was one of the last areas in the United States opened for homesteading. The area was bypassed by earlier homesteaders because of the high altitude and poor soil. The majority of those homesteading near Pie Town were refugees fleeing the Dust Bowl in Oklahoma and Texas, and they arrived because of the promise of free land. Some were relocated pinto bean farmers from drought stricken areas and others stayed because they ran out of gas and money and had nowhere else to go. By 1940, there were over two hundred families living on homesteads surrounding Pie Town.

Unknown travelers on Highway 60. Courtesy: Dorothy Cole Collection.

In Agnes Cleveland's book she describes the exodus that passed through Datil and Pie Town during the Great Depression, "I watched homesteaders as they trekked by. They came in family groups, in any sort of conveyance that would roll, their household furnishings piled high and overflowing with washtubs, baby buggies, chicken coops, wired to any anchorage that would hold."

Russell Lee, a photographer with the Farm Security Administration during the depression years described Pie Town in 1940, "When we arrived in Pie Town there wasn't much on that little street. There was a place to buy souvenirs and a community building on the same side of the street. On the right hand side was a filling station, not much, and the little hotel. On the other side of the street was Mr. Craig and Mr. Kelle's general store and café. We stayed in the hotel and it had two very small rooms. We had to cross Highway 60 to use the town privy as the hotel did not own its own privy."

The homesteaders living near Pie Town may have had little communication with those residing elsewhere, but they often got together at different community events. There were community sings, dances, literary meetings, church services and sewing circles. Lee described one of Pie Town's events,

"Next Sunday at Pie Town they are having a big, community sing with food and drinks as well; it will last all day."

Pie Town never regained the population of the homestead years, but the community remains a pleasant place to stop and have a piece of pie while enjoying the scenery of Highway 60. The 2010 census listed Pie Town's population as one hundred and eighty six residents.

The craze for gold and silver significantly contributed to the early development of the American frontier. Rumors and legends tell of buried treasure from the Superstition Mountains in Arizona to New Mexico's white sands. A local legend describes the mystery of the Lost Adams Diggings and a secret canyon of gold nuggets guarded by Nana and the Apache. Many researchers think the gold was initially found in the Pie Town area.

In 1864, a freighter named Adams lost most of his pack string to a group of Apache and barely made it to a Pima village near Casa Grande in Arizona. After Adams recited the story of his narrow escape to a cantina full of prospectors and outlaws, a man of mixed-blood named Gotch Ear told the group he knew of a canyon where a horse could be loaded in one day with gold nuggets.

An expedition of twenty-one men left Casa Grande in search of the canyon. Only the names of five men in the expedition are still known. They are Gotch Ear, Adams, John Brewer, Jack Davidson and John Sniverly. Gotch Ear was the only member of the expedition familiar with the country, and he led them down the Gila River for a few days eventually camping near Springerville, Arizona. The following morning, Gotch Ear pointed out two distinct peaks a hundred miles in the distance where the canyon full of gold was located.

For over a hundred years there has been much speculation on the identities of the two peaks. Were they Vetedo, Escondido or Horse Mountain near Quemado and Pie Town, or two peaks in the Zuni Mountains close to Gallo Peak and the Malpais? Was one of the peaks the Ladrone Mountains north of Socorro? Were the peaks in the Mogollon, San Mateo, Datil, Sawtooth or Magdalena Mountains? Or were they near Pie Town as many suspect? The only fact all accounts agree on is the gold was in a zig zag canyon opening into a grassy, park-like meadow.

After crossing an open plain, the group entered a canyon Gotch Ear gestured for the group to enter. Members of the expedition almost immediately "saw color" and stopped to pan for gold. They were overly excited by the amount of gold they found, and ignored Gotch Ear when he told them the gold nuggets were in the next canyon. Later, Gotch Ear was paid off and never heard from again. Some think he was killed by Nana shortly after leaving the canyon when he left the expedition panning for gold. Nana often had members of his band guard the canyon, although except for the discovery by settlers, the Apache did not appear overly concerned about the gold.

Soon after the expedition set up camp, Nana and thirty Apache warriors arrived and in fluent Spanish Nana told the group to not go beyond the falls at the end of the mountain range. The group agreed and continued prospecting and built a small, log cabin. Except for John Sniverly, the members of the expedition agreed to put all the gold they found into one container and hide under the fireplace in the cabin.

By the middle of September, the group was running low on provisions and six men under the command of John Brewer set out for a trading post in the malpais, a four day ride from their location. When the men were a day late returning, Adams and Davidson went in search of them and found five mutilated and lifeless bodies near the entrance to the canyon. After hiding the bodies, they returned to warn those in camp but heard the Apache already attacking the remaining members of the expedition.

The Apache killed the rest of the prospectors and burned the cabin. Adams and Davidson waited until after dark to make an attempt to reach the cabin, but it was smoldering and the fireplace too hot for them to try removing the gold. They decided to leave the canyon and return at a later date. They traveled by night and eventually arrived at an unidentified fort.

Jack Davidson returned to his home state of Ohio where he soon passed away. It was thought his knowledge of the treasure and its location was lost when he died. But, his daughter made his journal public in 1929 and a map showing the canyon with the gold. No one has come forward and admitted to finding the gold.

Adams headed for his family in California and disappeared for the next decade. He returned to New Mexico Territory in 1874 and searched for the gold until his death in 1886. He conducted extensive searches from

Springerville to the Zuni Mountains, in the Malpais, San Agustine Plains and along the Gila River. For many years he used Milligan Plaza now known as Reserve as his headquarters. He believed the fort where he had been rescued was near Reserve.

John Sniverly arrived in Pinos Altos after the attack with an array of impressive, gold nuggets he reportedly cashed in for thirteen thousand dollars. He said he found the gold one hundred and twenty five miles to the north near Pie Town. Unfortunately, he was killed in 1871 at his ranch near Prescott, Arizona. Sniverly probably had the best idea of the location of the gold, but if he ever returned to the location it was not documented.

More than likely, John Brewer either escaped with the gold or returned for it after the Apache left the canyon and then never told anyone about it. He was the only survivor who did not spend time searching for the gold afterwards. He never communicated with Adams or Davidson again thinking they had been killed by the Apache. Communication was not always reliable and the men came from different sections of the country. Later Brewer took his family to Mexico and became a prosperous and respected rancher in the area.

One-room schoolhouses once dotted the American frontier from Montana to New Mexico. One teacher organized lessons on all subjects and grade levels, and the students walked or rode horse-back to class. These early schools often had dirt floors, outdoor privies, and a hitching post or corral for horses. A teacher's residence was provided near the schoolhouse and in the 1920s teachers made between six hundred and eight hundred dollars a year. School was in session between Labor Day and April 15.

In 1923 there were twenty-one schools in Catron County with a total of eight hundred and five students. The school supcrintendent was Miss Deatron Campbell, and she traveled alone by buckboard to the area schools where she provided assistance to a largely, inexperienced staff of young teachers.

Clarice Reed, a teacher at the Divide School twelve miles south of Pie Town, left a description of her teaching days in the self-published book, *From the Top of the Mountain* by Kathryn McKee Roberts who grew up in Pie Town. She wrote, "The first morning of school, children came on horses and in wagons. I had twenty children and all eight grades. The men brought our wood, and the larger boys split and cut it. Water was drawn from a dug well. Each child brought their own cup and we had a dipper in the bucket to be used to fill their cups. We also had a wash pan so each child could wash before eating their lunches that had been brought from home."

If a teacher's residence was not provided, the teacher boarded with a family from the area. In some cases they "boarded round" meaning they lived with a different family from week to week or month to month. Clarice Reed paid twenty five dollars for room and board and her teaching salary was eighty five dollars a month.

The schoolhouse was an important part of the community and used for literary meetings, singings, church services, weddings, dances and for family gatherings. Reed described how the Divide School was used for several church services and wrote, "On Sundays there was always church in the schoolhouse. First the Church of Christ had their services and then the Baptists had theirs. It was more like a Bible study but it was great."

According to Robert's book, the school in Pie Town started in 1939, and the first teacher was Miss Grace Lucus. At first classes were held in the Farm Bureau Building. The county was unable to pay Miss Lucus, so those who had students in the school paid her in butter, chickens, pinto beans, eggs, milk or whatever they had. The county agreed to pay the teacher's wages the following year and to a school in Pie Town that remained in the Farm Bureau Building until 1947 when a four-room schoolhouse was completed.

Another school named Pipe Springs located three miles to the west of Alegra Mountain began in 1930. The first year the students sat on benches and used desks made of split logs. In 1936 there were enough students for both and elementary and high school.

Dorothy Bedinfeld, another teacher in Robert's book taught at the Sallie's Pine School and described her first day on the job. "There was a heating stove made of a big barrel, sitting in the middle of the room. I was provided with an old fashioned bell with a handle, with which I could call the children to class. There were no desks or seats for the young children, so we improvised. The building was furnished with many benches with backs that they had made for church services. These we turned around back to front. Out in the yard there were a great many log ends that had been sawed off while building the school. These log ends, the children and me carried in, placed by the benches and used for seats. So now we are equipped for school. We also had a blackboard."

14

Quemado, the Apache Indians and Champion Trick Rider Eleanor Williams

Judges stand at Quemado rodeo. Russell Lee Photograph.

The last town along Highway 60 before reaching the Arizona border is Quemado. The town was originally named Rio Quemado meaning burned stream in Spanish. When the first Spanish settlers arrived in the area from Belen, the ground appeared to have been recently burned. The settlers believed the Apache had set fire to the land adjacent to the stream.

Conflicting stories concerning the name persist though. Some early settlers attributed the name to ancient volcanic eruptions leaving the land with a scorched look. Other stories tell of an underground burning coal deposit adding to the appearance of the land. One story even points to an Apache chief who supposedly burned his hand in a campfire and afterwards the area was referred to as burned or scorched.

The community had a post office by 1886 but settlement was slow in the area due to Apache attacks. With Geronimo on the reservation and Victorio's band massacred in Mexico, ranchers and homesteaders began to move to the area. The Zuni Salt Lakes to the north and Quemado Lake to the south are popular recreation sites among locals and tourists.

In the 1880s, Baltazar Baca, one of the original settlers in Belen, moved his family to the Laguna Land Grant. Many families felt they were safer from Indian attacks in western Valencia County and the Arizona border country. These settlers would be the first in the Quemado area. Other settlers from Belen moved to Magdalena and Socorro making Belen a colonization center for the area. The Aragon family also from Belen founded the town of Aragon to the south. The Trujillos and Castillos settled in the Datil area. Belen became a mother colony for Catron, Guadalupe, Lincoln, Torrance and Valencia Counties.

The book *Quemado, New Mexico 250 Friendly people and a Few Old Crabs* written by Ruth Brown describes early Quemado. "The dirt road that went through Quemado was in the shape of a Z. At the bottom of the Z was old town. It had five or ten adobe houses and a filling station. The first settlers to come to the Quemado area in 1873 were the Francisco Padilla family." The part of Quemado considered old town soon had a store and post office as more and more settlers arrived in the area.

The newer section of the town was at the top of the Z. Most of the buildings were built on one side of the road and had false fronts. There were two general stores, three filling stations, the Sweazea Hotel and the Quemado Tavern. Located in the middle of the Z between the two sections of the town was the school.

Ira Sweazea, I.N. Curtis, Roger Candaleria and Ed Engle owned most of the businesses in early Quemado. Sweazea bought the old Francisco Padilla Ranch and a house in town that belonged to the Lucero family. The house had a porch along three sides and the rooms opened onto the porch and Sweazea turned the house into a hotel.

The Allison Tourist Court was a popular location for travelers, although business began slowly as Highway 60 would not be paved in this area until the 1950s. Brown explains how a cowboy came into the court one afternoon asking if he could take a shower, and this started a brisk showering business. Ranchers would come in from the country for an event and stop at the Allison Tourist Court to take a shower. The family made more money on showers than rooms when they first started the business.

The Apache conflict ended in New Mexico Territory with the surrender of Geronimo in 1886. Prior to this time the Black Range, San Mateos and Mogollon Mountains were the favorite haunts of Victorio and Nana. They were two Apache leaders considered the best guerilla fighters in the history of the Indian Wars.

Nana and Victorio were members of the Warm Springs or Mimbres band of the Chiricahua Apache Indian tribe. They often outmaneuvered and defeated their enemies with a fourth of their opponent's fighting force. Nana was Victorio's segundo or second lieutenant as well as his uncle.

Victorio's band ranged between the Sacramento and San Andres Mountains to the east and southwest into Arizona and Mexico. They were able to vanish into the mountains and disappear after a raid. They cached food and ammunition and it was next to impossible to apprehend them.

Victorio encouraged his band to accept reservation life at least twice but only remained a short time. In 1880 he left the reservation for good and escaped into the Mogollon Mountains where he killed miners and settlers between Mogollon, Cooney and Alma. Next, he stepped up his raids along the Rio Grande River. Victorio often attacked prospectors alone and those living in isolated settlements. He killed three men working the Rosedale Claim in the San Mateo Mountains, others working in mines at Kingston and then back along the San Francisco River near Reserve.

The ghost town of Patterson located to the south of Highway 60 was named after Richard Chase Patterson or R.C. He homesteaded land in the area and used a large rock on a hill close to his homestead as a makeshift fort during Apache raids. He stocked the location with food, water, guns and ammunition. In 1880, Patterson and his neighbors killed seventeen of Victorio's warriors while under siege.

Luck ran out for Victorio near Tres Castillos, Mexico in the fall of 1880 when the small band was massacred by a superior force of the Mexican army. Many historians believe Victorio's warriors killed themselves in order to not be taken as prisoners. Nana was scouting for supplies and ammunition and discovered the group after they were ambushed. Nana, in his seventies at the time, gathered the seventeen survivors of the band and headed into the Sierra Madre Mountains in Mexico in order to regroup and tend to the wounded.

As was the custom of the Apache, Nana and his warriors devised a revenge campaign. It would have been considered dishonorable to not avenge the death of a leader of Victorio's status. Nana's band crossed back across the border into the United States in January of 1881. They killed two miners near the mining camp of Chloride and wounded another. Later that month, they killed four more men on the Silver City & Mesilla Road. The band traversed over three thousand miles between Mescalero and El Paso; through the Black Range and Mogollon Mountains to the Ladrone Range north of Socorro and then back to the Mexican border.

The U.S. Cavalry never caught Nana, and the Apache won at least seven engagements against them with a fighting force of not more than fifteen men. When Nana crossed the Mexican border near Sonora in August of 1881, the cavalry was ordered to abandon chase. Nana had become an embarrassment to the U.S. Government. They hoped the Mexicans would take care of the problem as they had done with Victorio.

Nana joined forces with Geronimo and continued fighting for two more years. In 1883 he surrendered to General George Crook and was sent to the San Carlos Indian Reservation in Arizona. By 1885, Nana and Geronimo had left the reservation and escaped once again into Mexico.

Apache scouts were used to track down the last of the Chiricahua in 1886. This time the U.S. Government took no more chances with the Apache and shipped them, along with the scouts who had helped with the capture, first to Florida and then Alabama. Eventually they ended up at Fort Sill, Oklahoma where Nana died in 1896 at the age of ninety years old. He was still considered a prisoner of the United States.

Eleanor Williams, a champion trick and bronc rider moved to the Quemado area in the 1930s and started the Rising Sun Dude Ranch. She was born to wealthy Pittsburgh artists in 1906, but left her luxurious and elite lifestyle behind to become a champion trick rider for Ringling Brothers Barnum & Bailey Circus and rode bucking horses in Tim McCoy's Wild West Show.

Eleanor was introduced to western life in the 1920s when on vacation at Nan Hart's Montana dude ranch. She became enthralled with horses and outdoor life. She decided to have her own dude ranch one day. She would begin a correspondence with Nan Hart that chronicled her career as a trick and bronc rider plus her purchase and development of the Rising Sun Dude Ranch.

Women's trick and bronc riding were featured events in Wild West shows and rodeos the first forty years of the twentieth century. The event was cut at Madison Square Garden in 1941 and since has not returned to the traditional rodeo circuit. A few of the more famous lady bronc riders from this era were: Pearl Mason, Alice Greenough, Tad Lucas, Prairie Rose Henderson, Fannie Spears and a New Mexico cowgirl named Eleanor McClintock Williams.

In 1928, Eleanor attended a rodeo at Madison Square Garden in New York City and met her future husband a rodeo cowboy named Walter Heacock. Eleanor and Walter eloped two weeks later and joined a Wild West show bound for Chile. However they were stranded when the manager ran off with the gate money. Fortunately, they were able to find passage on a Japanese cargo ship and returned to the United States where they continued working the rodeo circuit.

In the 1930s, Walter and Eleanor had the opportunity to buy a three hundred acre ranch for $2.00 an acre adjacent to the Apache National Forest in New Mexico where they established the Rising Sun Dude Ranch. They worked on the ranch during the months they were not following the rodeo circuit.

In 1934, her six year marriage to Walter Heacock ended in divorce. Since Eleanor proved she had made most of the payments on the ranch, she was able to keep the property when her marriage ended. In order to continue paying off the debt on the ranch, she took a job with Ringling Brothers Barnum & Bailey Circus where she walked the tightrope and became a champion trick rider.

In a letter to Nan Hart dated February 15, 1936 Eleanor writes about the end of her first season as a trick rider, "We had to build charcoal fires in the dressing room to keep from freezing, and our necessary daily bucket baths were accomplished by shrieks and goose pimples. Even Jacksonville, Florida the next to last spot we played was plenty cold."

At the end of the 1936 season when the circus closed in Miami, Eleanor went back to winter quarters and picked up her trick horse Sonny Boy and her car and horse trailer. In the same letter she tells how she could hardly wait to get back to the ranch in New Mexico.

In her correspondence with Nan Hart, Eleanor reveals the rigor of circus life in the 1930s, "We were there (Miami, Florida) till the fourth of April, when we started our long trek northward by train," she wrote. "We were all in one train-horses, giraffes, lions, acrobats—even the man on the flying trapeze and honestly I thought that trip would never end."

The long rides on the train in-between shows were not always comfortable as described by Eleanor, "We were traveling at a third class freight rate, and fully half of the time en route was spent sitting on the railroad sidings waiting for the regular trains to whiz by. We had no chair cars of any description, and the Ringling Brothers Pullman bunks are all built to stay put and they don't turn into seats by the day."

She liked working for Ringling Brothers because they provided grooms for the horses and took care of them between performances. She wrote, "It is an easier life for me than I have been used to for years. Of course, during the show we really have to scramble, changing costumes, etc. but when the show is over we are free to rest or do anything we want to do."

During the 1938 season while working for Ringling Brothers she met her second husband, Earl Cline, a circus cowboy performing with the show. The marriage did not last long as Earl had a drinking problem and did not always help with the bills.

The couple joined Tim McCoy's Wild West Show in order to keep the dude ranch going. She wrote to Nan Hart, "This winter has been the most worrisome of any that I have ever known. It has been a nightmare of financial worry. With mounting bills and several debts, I finally got desperate this spring and took a job on a big Wild West show that opened in Chicago in April, riding bucking horses. Earl got connected with it too, as one of the assistant cashiers."

Tim McCoy would eventually go bankrupt because of the extravagance of his show. The show was intended to surpass the 101 and Buffalo Bill Cody shows. Riders came from everywhere: Argentina, Italy, Mexico, Australia, India, England and the United States.

The Clines decided to leave the show when Eleanor had an accident while performing. Her horse pulled away from the pickup man, then reared back hitting her in the face. The impact of the horse's head knocked her unconscious and drove one of Eleanor's teeth through her upper lip cracking her cheekbone. They received a letter from New Mexico the same day as the accident informing them the dude ranch had been mismanaged by the couple they had hired as caretakers.

They decided to leave the show and return home as soon as possible. Eleanor writes about their plans to return to New Mexico. "That was the first day of the Washington engagement, and I drew out what money I had coming to me that night, as did Earl, and we left the next day. And what a break for us that we did, as that was Monday, and Wednesday creditors closed down the luckless show and it went into the hands of receivers, and everyone got five dollars apiece."

When the Clines returned to New Mexico, they found the caretakers had charged eighty-five dollars in unauthorized food and feed for the livestock. They had also butchered a yearling steer and sold part of the meat, cleaned out their pantry and neglected the livestock.

Eleanor decided to remain on the ranch and oversee things while Earl looked for rodeo work in California. It was not easy for her as described to Nan in another letter, "I am holding things down here and running the school bus with my car for $40.00 a month," she wrote. "That isn't great wealth, but it keeps us going." But Earl and Eleanor would divorce when he returned from California.

In 1940 Eleanor met Frank Williams, the cowboy she would spend the rest of the life with. He was a rancher from Magdalena who leased the ranch next door and they soon began seeing one another. She was excited about meeting Frank as expressed in her letter to Nan, "Fate decreed that he should fall in love with me and me with him. This is the end of the trail."

Frank had grown up in New Mexico, and his father was an Indian fighter and scout for wagon trains traveling west. Eleanor added, "He has never known anything but ranch life and has been the foreman of some the biggest cow outfits around this country."

Eleanor and Frank operated a part-time dude ranch and full-time working cattle ranch together for the remainder of their lives with the help of their children and grandchildren until their deaths in the 1970s. Their descendants continue living on the ranch near Quemado now known as the Williams' Ranch.

Before her obsession with the rodeo circuit, Eleanor had considered a career in art. She attended Carnegie Tech and the Art Students League in New York City. In later years, she painted ranch scenes and ran for the New Mexico Senate.

Eleanor was inducted into the Cowgirl Hall of Fame in 1986 for her contributions to rodeo and western life. Her biography reads, "Eleanor's life epitomized that of the strong, independent western woman. She became a champion trick rider, performing on the rodeo circuit, Wild West shows and circuses. She purchased and built a ranch during the Depression, raised five children, ran for the NM Senate, was a published writer and became a recognized artist."

In the 1930s, Quemado was described as the Rodeo Center of New Mexico. A group of rodeo celebrities often practiced together at Eleanor and Walter Heacock's dude ranch south of town that included Donald Nesbitt, the former World Champion All-Around Cowboy and Dick Griffith a well-known trick rider of the era. Walter's brothers Steve and Chuck also participated in these practices and they traveled the rodeo circuit together.

Dick Griffith trick riding. Author's collection.

Quemado has grown a little during the past decades but remains a small, ranching community. The town has a state police stationed in town, the U.S. Forest Service district office, senior citizen center and fire department. The nearby Quemado Lake and the Gila National Forest provides recreational opportunities during the summer months and the area is known for elk and deer hunting. Quemado had a population of two hundred and twenty eight residents in the 2010 census.

15

Landmarks along Highway 60

The Llano Estacado or Staked Plains greeted railroad men and homesteaders arriving on New Mexico's east side at the turn of the twentieth century. The Comanche and Apache Indians lived and hunted on the Llano Estacado for centuries before the arrival of the railroad and remains of the Clovis and Folsom sites are evidence of even earlier inhabitants at Black Water Draw and at Folsom, New Mexico near the Colorado border.

The Llano Estacado is considered part of the flattest part of the United States. The Llano (as it is called by the locals) reaches from the Canadian River in the north to Edwards Plateau to the south. The Pecos River borders the semi-arid tableland to the east.

In 1902 the El Paso & Northeastern Railroad finished what they referred to as the Arrow Route. It ran between El Paso and Santa Rosa where it connected to the Rock Island Line. To the south of Highway 60 is the small town of Duran. The town became a division point on the route and at its peak had a population of three hundred people.

Continuing westward small peaks and mesas served as landmarks for early travelers making their way through the isolated country. Duran Mesa can be seen for at least a hundred miles with the Pino Mountains silhouetted in the background where the ghost town of Pinos Wells is located. The first settlers in the once booming town were the Lucero, Chavez and Salas families. Antonio Salas had two water wells west of town near two pine trees and the community assumed the name of Pinos Wells.

The community was a stage stop in the 1880s on the Santa Fe Trail running between Santa Fe and White Oaks. The town provided water, food and lodging. It was one of the few sites where water was available in those days. At the town's peak there were two stores, two saloons, a rooming house and the first post office in the area. The town reached a population of four hundred in 1914 and by 1939 only ninety-one people remained.

Between Vaughn and Mountainair along high points on the route the Sangre de Cristo Mountains near Santa Fe can be seen on the northern horizon. The mountain range is considered the southernmost sub-range of the Rocky Mountains. The range reaches from southern Colorado to northern New Mexico. The Spanish named the mountain after the reddish colors on the mountain at sunset reminding them of the "Blood of Christ" thus supplying the name.

On a clear day, Rowe Mesa near Las Vegas and Interstate 25 is seen near Villanueva State Park along the Pecos River on Highway Three. The Barlow & Sanderson Line had a stage stop near the park at the turn of the twentieth century.

The Gallinas Mountains, south of the Pino Range rise to an elevation of over eight thousand feet at Gallinas Peak where the U.S. Forest Service staffs Gallinas Fire Lookout during fire season. The small range has suffered devastating fires since the 1950s but is a popular hunting area for elk and turkey.

The mountains are surrounded by large ranches and the town of Corona to the east. In the 1880s the Las Vegas Trail ran east of the range between Las Vegas and White Oaks. Mail and supplies came over the route supplying the bustling, mining trade.

A military fort was once located south of Gallina Spring in the early 1800s and staffed by the U.S. Fifth Cavalry a regiment of buffalo soldiers. Their duties were to protect travelers on the Las Vegas Trail and ranchers from the Apache and outlaw gangs plus they provided the only law and order in an extremely lawless region. The Buffalo Soldiers were largely responsible for the little order that was had in Lincoln County during these years.

The Pedernal Hills near Clines Corners are distinct from the east as their peaks rise above the plains. Clines Corners and Interstate 40 are located directly north of the hills. For those traveling the endless stretch of highway making up Interstate 40 Clines Corners has provided a place to take a break from the road, fill up with gas and have a bite to eat for the past eighty-one years. Roy Cline, its first proprietor did not remain in one location for long but left his name for the roadside business he established in 1934.

When Cline first arrived at the location of his new filling station at Clines Corners highway construction crews were camping on the land he had leased. They were preparing the road for paving with a WWI Liberty truck and pull blade and living in a canvas tent in the back of an old truck.

In 1937 the highway department decided to reroute and rename the highways where Cline's business sat. The road known as the Santa Rosa Cutoff was moved and renamed U.S. Highway 285. Cline had to move to remain in business and jacked up his buildings and hauled them to the new location.

Highway construction crews prepared Route 66 for paving with Caterpillar tractors referred to as crawling cats because they ran on tracks instead of wheels. The cats pulled six-foot blades used for clearing the road. Caliche was used as a base for the highway and soon crews had the road paved all the way to Moriarty. The paving of Route 66 cut off one hundred miles from the original route, bypassed Santa Fe and headed in a straight line to Albuquerque.

Continuing to the west, the Manzano and Sandia Mountains appear on the horizon. Life was not easy on the east side of the Manzano Mountains in the 1820s when Spanish colonists from Tome began herding their sheep on the vast, uninhabited plains east of the mountains. The Apache and Navajo Indians had controlled the land for over a hundred and forty years and would not easily relinquish that control as the Spanish attempted colonizing the area.

The Spanish had settled near Torreon and Manzano in the 1600s but were forced to leave during the Pueblo Revolt of 1680. The Puebloans united under the leadership of Pope from the San Juan Pueblo and pushed the Spanish out of New Mexico. Twelve years later due to internal bickering among the Puebloans the Spanish were able to return and take Santa Fe without firing a shot.

Those first Spanish settlers to return to New Mexico built their settlements in the style of a plazuela or fortified town with walls surrounding the community and a torreon for protection. A torreon was normally a round structure with portholes for shooting where the settlers could lock themselves inside and wait out an Apache attack. During this era, this type of structure was common as it was a way the settlers found they could survive Apache raids.

Over a century later, Bartolome Baca was the first Spanish colonist to request a grant of land near the mountains. Baca built his ranch at Torreon Springs at the former estancia (ranch) of Joseph Nieto. Nieto's old torreon would later give the town its name. Baca encouraged other colonists to petition for land and in 1823 Manzano became the first permanent settlement east of the mountains since the revolt.

Water, supplies and ammunition were stored inside the torreon and during an Apache raid the women and children remained inside while the men fought off the Apache outside. Early Manzano was built as a walled fortress and someone was always on guard watching for an attack while the others worked. The first Spanish settlers were a tough and determined group.

0951   FORT MANZANA, NEAR MOUNTAINAIR, N. M. ON THE BELEN CUT-OFF.   FRED HARVEY.

Torreon and Fort at Manzano. Courtesy: Dorothy Cole Collection.

Apache and Navajo raids were almost constant for the colonists between the years of 1822 and 1833. The Comanche also invaded the area from Texas and often raided settlers at Tome yet traded with them during trade fairs.

Once Manzano was established, members of the Lucero family moved with a group of settlers to the ruins at Quarai, while another group headed by the Sisneros (Cisneros) family settled at Abo near the ancient Tompiro site. At both locations a plazuela or fortified settlement was quickly constructed.

The Sisneros group built their houses close together with portholes and a torreon connected. They also built a wall around the settlement in order to keep the animals from being abducted and to give the women and children further protection.

The Lucero group used stones from the pueblo to build a walled area east of the mission with a torreon and corrals for the animals. It seems, the colonists received permission to build a church at Manzano, but the Lucero faction were not in agreement and started a church at the ruins at Quarai. The church was never finished because those at Manzano petitioned for it to remain there.

The mission church at Quarai still had its choir loft and roof in the late 1820s when the Spanish settled at the site. The group used the church as a burial ground for the growing number killed during Apache and Navajo raids. Unfortunately for the group the remaining timbers in the roof, choir loft and lintels of the church were burned by the Apache in either 1829 or 1830.

In September of 1829, those residing in Manzano petitioned the Territorial Deputation of Tome for a community land grant. The original land grant requested a tract of land that included land between Torreon to the north and Abo on the south, from the base of the Manzano Mountains to Las Humanas Mesa near Willard.

The Deputation considered the requested piece of land too large and instead granted a smaller grant located between Mountainair and Quarai but excluded Abo. This decision would affect the Sisneros family and other settlers at Abo, and they would be forced to abandon the site in the 1830s and return to Manzano. The group at Quarai held out a little longer but eventually abandoned and returned to the relative safety of Manzano.

The relentless attacks by the Apache, Navajo and Comanche slowed down the colonization movement planned by the Spanish settlers for another thirty years and by that time New Mexico had become part of the United States. In the 1860s, the Sisneros family once again moved to Abo and the Lucero and Gonzales families returned to Quarai where they would establish the community of Punta de Agua. Descendants of these same original Spanish colonists continue to live in the area settled by their ancestors.

South of Highway 60 is Chupadera Mesa where the Gran Quivira Unit of Salinas Pueblo Missions National Monument is located. For close to two centuries a gold myth has persisted at Gran Quivira. Does the name Quivira have anything to do with this misconception? Quivira was the name of the mythical city of gold Spanish explorer Francisco Vasquez de Coronado searched for all the way to Kansas yet never found? Or was there buried treasure or even gold bells hidden within the walls of the old ruins at one time?

During the century and a half the site remained abandoned it was often used as a camping location for those traveling between settlements. Prior to the 1880s, there were few towns and roads along New Mexico's east side. Those traveling between Las Vegas, Santa Fe, Lincoln and Albuquerque had few choices but to camp along their route. The old ruins provided the perfect location to get out of the wind, explore the ruins and search for buried treasure.

William and Clara Corbin arrived in New Mexico Territory in 1882 after investing all their money in a railroad scheme and then losing everything in the financial crash of 1893. The Corbins read about the treasure supposedly buried at Gran Quivira and in an attempt to regain their money decided to search for the treasure. They were granted a homestead claim of one hundred and sixty acres including the Mission of San Buenaventura where they thought the treasure was located.

William had served during the Civil War and upon his discharge he decided to head west. He left his first wife and children back in New York and never returned. He wrote asking his wife for a divorce but did not receive one and instead married Clara Ball in 1874 in Ohio and later moved to New Mexico Territory.

By the time the Corbins arrived at Gran Quivira, Clara was legally blind and gradually losing her eyesight. William attached guidelines through-out the mission, so Clara could find her way from room to room without his assistance. They set up a canvas tent in the mission and began excavating for the treasure they hoped to find there.

William was twenty years older than Clara and when he started to have health issues, they traveled to Albuquerque to seek medical attention. William passed away in 1898, leaving Clara behind with little money and means of support. Unknown to her, his legal wife back in New York would receive his Civil War pension, which Clara was counting on to get by until she found the treasure.

Clara began giving lectures in Albuquerque on topics about the treasure and history of Gran Quivira in an attempt to support herself. She also bought a typewriter, which were not common on the frontier during these years, and began typing letters for her neighbors at Gran Quivira. She wrote a book titled: *La Gran Quivira, a Musical Mystery: Opera Historique, A Romanza in Five Acts with Overture, Prelude and Interlude* which she would self-publish in 1904. Clara began selling subscriptions for her book and traveled by rail to Los Angeles and other cities hoping to sell enough copies to return to Gran Quivira and continue excavating for treasure.

She continued to seek funds to excavate Gran Quivira but would pass away before she found the treasure or made any money off her book. She passed away in Los Angeles, California in 1913. The Museum of New Mexico bought Corbin's homestead in 1914 and included it within the boundary of Gran Quivira National Monument.

Highway 60 continues past Mountainair and through Abo Pass on its way to the Rio Grande River and Interstate 25. At the summit of the mountain range is Blue Springs. The business was first built by Maxmillion Miranda as a café and bar. Miranda put the elephant out front in an attempt to attract business and at one time there was a small rhino next to the elephant. The location has been a restaurant, bar, dance hall and home. It is currently no longer open for business.

The small settlement or "wide spot in the road" of Bernardo is the final location on the east side of Highway 60. At this junction, the highway turns south and joins Interstate 25 until reaching Socorro and the Magdalena exit where it once again turns west on its way to the Arizona border.

Bernardo was named after a friend of Belen merchant John Becker. For most of its history the location was made up of a convenience store, gas station and bar but is now a private residence. The Kiva RV Park & Horse

Motel, located on the west side of the Interstate, is currently all that remains of Bernardo.

Robert and Diane Wiltshire have owned the RV Park since 1999. They planted trees, added horse boarding facilities and trail rides making the location a small oasis in the desert. Robert manages the park while Diane is in charge of the horses and trail rides. She is a certified riding instructor for both adults and children.

For those traveling by RV or camper, it is a nice location to spend the night or a few days while exploring Highway 60. The nearby mountains, Rio Grande River, the ghost town of Riley and San Lorenzo Canyon provide interesting day trips. Horses can be boarded daily, weekly or monthly at the Horse Motel and there are trail riding opportunities in the area.

West of Bernardo is the Ladrone Mountains. The range of mountains has served as a New Mexico landmark since the late 1500s when Don Juan de Onate brought the first European settlers up the El Camino Real. In the 1880s the mountains served as a hideout for outlaws plus Apache and Navajo renegades and nicknamed Thieves Mountain. Stories have survived hinting at Civil War cannons and buried gold.

To the south and east of Interstate 25 and Highway 60 is the village of La Joya. Originally, it was the site of a Piro Indian pueblo and named Sevilleta by the Spanish, because it reminded them of Seville in Spain. During the boom years of travel and trade on the El Camino Real, La Joya was an important staging area for southbound caravans. The settlement was the last fortified community before reaching El Paso.

By the seventeenth century attacks by the Apache and Comanche had caused the pueblo at La Joya to be abandoned. In 1880 the area was resettled by the Robledos and Romero families and the community was referred to as La Joya de Seveilleta. At various times, the settlement was also named La Jolla, Ranchitos de la Holla and El Jollal.

The Ladrone Mountains are administered by the BLM and U.S. Fish and Wildlife Service. In 1973 the Campbell family donated land to the Nature Conservancy and the land became the Seveilleta National Wildlife Refuge. The refuge reaches from the Ladrone Mountains to the Los Pinos Range near Blue Springs to the east.

In 1862, Confederate forces under General Sibley invaded New

Mexico Territory from Texas during the Civil War. After a reasonably easy victory over Union troops at Fort Craig near the river crossing of Valverde, the Southerners continued north following the Rio Grande River to Albuquerque.

A month later, Sibley's soldiers were defeated by a detachment of Colorado volunteers during the Battle of Glorietta near present-day Pecos. The entire Confederate supply train was destroyed with at least seventy wagons set ablaze and over five hundred mules and horses lost. The Confederates escaped with little more than the clothes they were wearing and their cannons. Sibley abandoned half of his artillery in Albuquerque before following the Rio Grande River south to Mesilla where another supply train waited.

After a confrontation with Union forces under General Canby at Peralta north of Belen, the Confederates crossed to the west side of the Rio Grande. Canby's troops continued marching on the east side, and the two armies kept the other in sight until camping for the night near the Ladrone Mountains.

Later that night, the Confederates secretly broke camp and quietly moved toward the Rio Salado River. They abandoned additional cannons and equipment between the river and Magdalena. Although most of the cannons were found, rumors of hidden gold and cannons have persisted ever since.

In 1898, the mountains were a temporary hideout of two Texas outlaws named Bronco Bill and Kid Johnson. They belonged to a larger gang of cattle thieves and train robbers plaguing southern New Mexico and west Texas.

On May 23, after concealing their horses two miles south of Belen, the two robbers walked to the depot, bought tickets and boarded the train. They forced the engineer at gunpoint to stop the train. They used dynamite to open a Wells-Fargo safe holding twenty five thousand dollars and escaped in the direction of the Ladrone Mountains.

The sheriff's office in Los Lunas was notified of the robbery, and two deputies named Vigil and Bustamante went in pursuit. They found the trail of the robbers skirting the edge of the Ladrone Range in the direction of the Navajo community of Alamo. A group of Apache and Navajo Indians informed the deputies of two, heavily-armed men ahead on the trail. The group decided to camp for the evening and attempt apprehending the outlaws the following morning.

At sunup Vigil, Bustamante and two of the Apache saw a small, camp-fire coming up near the base of the Ladrone Mountains. They were able to approach without the outlaws noticing. When Vigil tried to read them their rights, they shot and killed him. They also killed Bustamante and one of the Apache before escaping. The remaining Apache was able to get away and warn those living in Alamo.

Over a year later, Wells-Fargo agents tracked Bronco Bill and Kid Johnson to a cave near Springerville, Arizona. During the gunfight that fol-lowed, Kid Johnson was killed and Bronco Bill badly wounded. He served time in the New Mexico Territorial Prison for his crimes, and upon his release worked for a rancher in the southwest corner of the territory where he fell off a windmill and died.

Magdalena's Original Main Street. Author's Collection.

To the Southwest of the Magdalena Mountains is the San Mateo Range. West of the mountains are the San Agustine Plains, where the Very Large Array (VLA) has antennas that study and relate computer information on the night time skies. The VLA consists of twenty seven radio antennas with each antenna reaching twenty five feet in diameter. The site is at an elevation of seven thousand feet.

West of the San Agustine Plains is the small, town of Datil on the Continental Divide where Highway 60 intersects with NM 12 and the towns of Aragon, Luna and Reserve. The town of Aragon, located on the Tularosa River northeast of Reserve began its history as Fort Tularosa. The fort was originally the site of the Warm Springs or Mimbres Apache Indian Agency between 1872 and 1874. When the Apache were removed the fort was abandoned.

Susan Lee relates the following story about the ghost of Fort Tularosa in her book, *These Also Served*. She writes, "My uncle told me about the time he encountered a ghost at the fort. When the army moved out of the country, the fort was used for camping by travelers."

She wrote, "The old fort had been built with a long hallway through the center with rooms along each side and a porch extending across the front of the building. When my uncle decided to spend the night there one night he turned his horse loose in a small pasture, took his saddle and blankets into the first room he came to, and after eating a meager meal, went to bed early as he had ridden many miles and was tired so was soon asleep."

Later, he was awakened by the sound of a horse and rider. He was not concerned at first, because people often used the old fort for camping. He clearly heard a rider dismount, remove his saddle and throw it on the front porch. He heard him slap his horse on the rump. Then he heard someone dragging a saddle into the hall.

He yelled out to let his visitor know he was in the first room but heard only silence in reply. He opened the door and the hallway was empty, no saddle, no cowboy and no horse grazing in the pasture outside. He looked in all the rooms finding them all empty.

It was then he had an eerie feeling realizing he had heard the ghost. He quickly found his horse, loaded his gear and went on his way. Similar stories were often related by travelers visiting the old fort while it remained standing.

The Mogollon Mountains are often distinct on the southern horizon while driving Highway 60. An interesting settler from Reserve was August

Kiehne who drove a herd of cattle into Catron County from Texas in 1884. He settled near Reserve establishing his ranch headquarters and the square and compass brand. Keihne was no stranger to cattle drives, as he worked for others trailing cattle while a teenager and was later in charge of his own drives. While on one of these drives he met Sally Hurst in Dodge City, Kansas. They were soon married and later had four children.

According to Susan Lee in her book *These Also Served*, Kiehne went on his first cattle drive in 1869 and helped trail three thousand head from Texas to California. Shortly after starting the drive, the group was attacked along the Pecos River by Comanche Indians. They were able to elude the Comanche, although one of their men was killed.

In the 1870s Kiehne worked for the U.S. Government supplying cattle for Sioux Indian Reservations in the Dakotas. After delivering one herd of cattle, he was confronted by Sitting Bull and his warriors. The Sioux chief wanted additional horses; and when Kiehne refused and tried to leave, Sitting Bull grabbed the horse's bridle. Kiehne was eventually able to parley with the group, and they left with most of the horses.

Cattle rustling, a major problem when Kiehne first moved to Catron County was a profitable enterprise for those operating outside the law. Lee describes an incident between rustlers and Kiehne near Reserve, "Kiehne and Uncle Bill Jones had a fight with rustlers. They came upon them trying to get off with a bunch of cattle. Ten men were killed and the rustlers defeated."

Lee quotes an interview with Kiehne in her book, "In those days the man who was the quickest with the six-shooter and the best shot was the one to survive. The only law was force. To kill a man in what was considered a justifiable fight was treated as a closed incident, but to steal a steer invited trouble for the thief; if caught, he was the guest of a necktie party."

Another settlement in the Mogollon Mountains to the south is Glenwood. The Bush family was instrumental in the early settlement of Glenwood and Catron County. Susan Lee describes the Bush Ranch in the book *These Also Served* and writes, "At an early point in the settlement of the Mogollon country the Bush Ranch, as it was then known was a familiar landmark and an objective point to the prospector, miner and stockman."

Discoveries of gold and silver in the Mogollon Mountains near

Cooney, Alma, Mogollon and Graham and other mining communities led to the development of Glenwood. Southwestern New Mexico was isolated in the 1870s and largely unsettled because of relentless attacks by the Apache, and the Bush Ranch provided a safer place to camp for miners and others traveling between settlements.

Glenwood claims to be the site of the first powered airplane flight in New Mexico. In 1909, Doc Rowe the local stage stop owner built a plane in the big barn on the original Bush Ranch. The plane was flown by an Austrian named George Quflea on Whitewater Mesa sometimes referred to as Airplane Mesa (on older maps) near Glenwood. The flying machine was built with a fuselage and five cylinder engine, a wooden frame and linen wings resembling steam-ship propellers.

Charles Walsh is actually credited with flying the first powered airplane in New Mexico. He flew a Curtiss biplane at the New Mexico Territorial Fair in 1911. He kept his plane in the air from the fairgrounds to the Barelas Bridge, then east to the railroad tracks and northwest across Robinson Park. The following year he died in an airplane crash in New Jersey. If the date can be verified, Rowe's plane beat Walsh by two years.

The village of Luna, located near the Arizona border was originally part of the sheep empire of Salomon Luna. He was a political force during New Mexico's territorial days and the grandson of Don Domingo de Luna, cousin of the Duke of Albuquerque and the first Luna to settle in what is now New Mexico.

Salamon Luna began his political career in Valencia County and later served on the National Republican Committee from New Mexico Territory. He was most often referred to as the largest sheep baron in the territory. Luna, like other large ranchers of the era often claimed the land by occupation. This would cause problems when the area was opened for homesteading.

Luna passed away during mysterious circumstances while overseeing the dipping of his sheep on the ranch of Montague Stevens near Horse Springs in 1912. His body was discovered partially decomposed in a sheep dipping vat. At first, murder and suicide were considered, but his death was eventually ruled an accident although many disagreed with the verdict.

In 1881 Melvin Swapp trailed a herd of cattle from Utah to Cliff. He decided to return the following year and settle with his widowed mother, brothers and several friends. The group laid out the town site of Luna. Since the country was the homeland of the Apache, the group decided to build a fort first. The fort was equipped with supplies and ammunition and a well dug inside. Later, they built cabins with porthole surrounding the fort.

In the beginning, the settlers had more problems with Salomon Luna than they did with the Apache. When they first arrived, they made a trade with Luna's sheepherders for their squatter's rights and they avoided problems by trading horses and cows for the use of the land.

Reserve, located along the San Francisco River is the county seat of Catron County and originally settled in the 1870s. The town was first called Upper Frisco Plaza and then shortened to merely Frisco. In later years, the community was referred to as Milligan Plaza and Milligan after an infamous saloon owner and merchant. The name Reserve was suggested after the creation of the U.S. Forest Reserves and a ranger headquarters built near the community. The Mogollon Mountains overshadow Reserve and Glenwood to the south as they wind through the arid landscape near the Gila River.

While driving Highway 60 between Pie Town and Quemado the mountain range to the south is Mangas Mountain. The mountain range is named after Mangas Colorados or Red Sleeves, a respected Apache leader. His death occurred near Pinos Altos to the south in 1863. After coming in under a white flat and in good faith, Mangas was later tormented by soldiers and when he protested they shot and killed him.

After his murder, Orson Squire Flower, a phrenologist-lecturer had the head of the great leader severed from his body and boiled out his skull to use in his lectures; his body was thrown in a nearby ditch afterwards. The disrespect showed the Apache chief caused "bad blood" between the tribe and soldiers for the next thirty years. The Apache were further incensed when miners and settlers continued moving into the area and disrupting their way of life.

Portions of the Black Range on the Gila National Forest are seen along the route before reaching the Arizona border and the White Mountains and the continuation of Highway 60 to California.

Highway 60 remains an isolated route, an alternative route, the route travelers take when they want to slow down and enjoy the scenery. Herds of elk are often seen near Pie Town and Datil and it is not uncommon to see cowboys moving cattle from one range to the other. The land has not changed that much since the Apache inhabited the area and there is still a feeling of the pioneer spirit that helped settle the land over a hundred years earlier.

If you are short on time and have to drive straight through, take at least fifteen minutes and stop in one of the ghost towns along the route and explore the history. Take a photograph or two and observe land unchanged by the passage of time. Highway 60 might be considered one of the more lonely routes in the state, but the history of the area is fascinating and waiting for someone to stop and explore.

The romantic days of train travel have passed. Most of the train depots are closed, the Harvey Houses boarded up or demolished and the Harvey Girls a faint memory. But, during their day they were the most popular places to have a good meal on the American frontier. Mabel and Lillian are pictured on the roof of the Los Chavez Harvey House in Vaughn while taking a break from their duties in 1918.

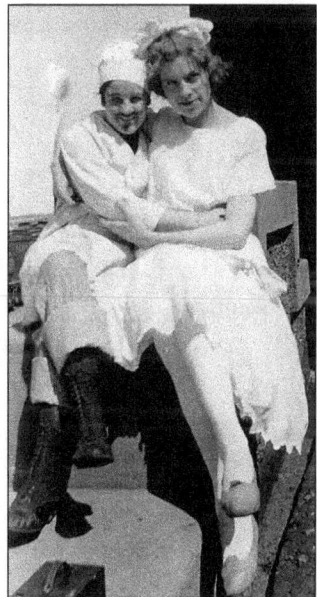

Vaughn Harvey Girls in 1918.
Courtesy: Belen Harvey House Museum.

Bibliography and Sources

Archuleta, Phil and Holden, Sharyl S. *Traveling New Mexico*. Santa Fe: Sunstone Press, 2004.

Ball, Eve. *In the Days of Victorio*. Tucson, Arizona: The University of Arizona Press, 1970.

Black, Johnathan. *Curry County, New Mexico*. Johnathon Black, 2013.

Brown, Ruth. *Quemado, New Mexico*. Las Cruces, New Mexico, 2007.

Bryant, Keith. *History of the Atchison, Topeka & Santa Fe Railroad*. New York: Macmillian Publishing Company, 1974.

Burr, Baldwin. *Belen*. Charleston, South Carolina: Arcadia Publishing, 2013.

Burroughs, Jean. *Roosevelt County History and Heritage*. Portales, New Mexico: Bishop Printing Company, 1975.

Celebrating One Hundred Years of Frontier Living. Published by Magdalena Old Timer's Association, 1994.

Chavez, Tibo and Espinosa, Bilbert. *El Rio Abajo*. Albuquerque: Espinosa & Wald.

Cleveland, Agnes Morley. *No Life for a Lady*. Lincoln: University of Nebraska Press, 1941.

Ernst, Donna. *Sundance, My Uncle*. College Station, Texas: Creative Publishing Company, 1992.

Flores, Daniel. *It Happened in Vaughn Stories About a New Mexico Railroad Town*, self-published, 2012.

French, William. *Recollections of a Western Ranchman*. Silver City, New Mexico: High Lonesome Books, 1928.

Henderson, Ester. *US Coast US 60. Arizona Highway Magazine*. Garden City, New York: Anchor Books Doubleday and Company, 1984.

Hurt, Wesley. *Manzano: A Study of Community Disorganization*. Master's Thesis, 1941.

Irving, David. *Vicious Explosion Rocked Tolar Sixty Years Ago, Clovis News Journal*, January 4, 2004.

Ivy, James E. *In the Midst of Loneliness The architectural History of Salinas Missions National Monument Historic Structure Report*. South Cultural Resource Center, 1988.

Julyan, Robert. *The Place Names of New Mexico*. Albuquerque: University of New Mexico Press, 1998.

Lee, Susan. *These Also Served*. Los Lunas, New Mexico: Susan E. Lee, 1960.

Lekson, Stephen. *Nana's Raid: Apache Warfare in Southern New Mexico*. El Paso: the University of Texas at El Paso: Texas Western Press, 1987.

Meltzer, Richard. *Harvey Houses of the Southwest*. Arcadia Publishing, 2008.

Metz, Leon. *The Shooters*. El Paso, Texas: Mangan Books, 1986.

Mulhouse, John. *City of Dust Blog*.

Murphy, Dan. *Salinas Pueblo Missions: Abo, Quarai and Gran Quivira*. Tucson: Western National Parks Association.

Poling-Kempes, Leslie. *The Harvey Girls: Women Who Operated the West*. New York: Paragon House, 1980.

Pounds, Robert. *Santa Fe Depots, the Western Lines*. Dallas: Kachina Press, 1984.

Roberts, Kathryn McKee. *From the Top of the Mountain Pie Town, New Mexico and Neighbors!* Published by Roger Coffin, 1990.

Stanley, F. *The Clovis, New Mexico Story*. Pep, Texas, 1969.

Stanley, F. *The Taiban, New Mexico Story*. Pep, Texas, 1969.

Stanley, F. *The Tolar, New Mexico Story*. Pep, Texas, 1967.

Stanley, F. *The Yeso, New Mexico Story*. Pep, Texas, 1969.

Stevens, Montague. *Meet Mr. Grizzly*. Albuquerque: University of New Mexico Press, 1944.

Thrapp, Dan. *Victorio and the Mimbres Apache*. Norman, Oklahoma: University of Oklahoma Press, 1974.

Torrance County History. Published by Torrance County Historical Society, 1979.

Willard, Willard, Willard. Published by Willard Centennial Committee, 2010.

Personal Interview with Carrie Lindsay, October 2007.

Personal Interview with Bob and June McLaughlin, October 2007.

Personal Interview with Helen Lavell, January 2015.

Personal Interview with Charlie Panebouef and Yvonne Hindi. February 2015.

Personal Interview with June McLaughlin, February 2015.

Personal Interview with Robert Wiltshire, February 2015.

Personal Interview with Paul Strong, February 2015.

www.ingramcontent.com/pod-product-compliance
Lightning Source LLC
Chambersburg PA
CBHW052136270326
41930CB00012B/2910